The Keys To The Kingdom

A Study of Natural Law: The Nine Laws
of the Cycles of Life

Rev. Terry Ryan

Body, Mind & Spirit / Spiritualism

The Keys To The Kingdom

A Study of Natural Law: The Nine Laws of the Cycles of Life

by Rev. Terry Ryan

© 2021 Reverend Terry Ryan
Chesterfield, IN USA
www.RevTerryRyan.com

Cover design by: Elle Phillips
Edited by: Judy Thorburn
Rev. Ryan's headshot by: Maurice W. Sanders

Personal Dynamics Publishing
www.PersonalDynamicsPublishing.com

ISBN: 978-0-9890889-6-1

About the Cover

In the writings of the ancient world, many documents speak of a legendary teacher of metaphysics by the name of Hermes Trismegistus (Trismegistus means 'three times greatest', referring to the respect and esteem he was held in). He is thought to have lived in ancient Egypt, although the exact time frame is somewhat vague. Some texts mention he was thought to be the same entity as the Egyptian god Thoth. In any event, he is credited with being the father of many of today's great sciences, such as astrology, astronomy, mathematics, chemistry, and many others. His relevance in this book is because he is considered to be the founder of what we know today as *Natural Law*, demonstrated in the Seven Hermetic Principles (described later).

In Greek mythology, the god Hermes was considered to be the messenger of the Gods. Given all that Hermes Trismegistus was said to have brought forth in the way of great teachings, and the similarity in names, it is likely they are one and the same, with the Greeks also considering this teacher to be of great importance. If so, how appropriate that he might be the *messenger of the Gods*. The Spirit world has always sent forth to the earth plane advanced souls to help guide and shape the progress of mankind.

The Medallion of Hermes: The Medallion is the only one in existence and was created by a Michigan jewelry craftsman. It is a contemporary metaphysical symbol describing the relationship between God the Creative Force, the Spirit world, and the physical world. Look closely at the Medallion; you will see three distinct sections. The first is the key and the large orb, representing the Cosmos. The second, the wings and dragonfly, symbolize the Spirit world. The third section with the gear, watch movement, and smaller orb, represents the physical world.

The Key: The key is symbolic of the Source of all knowledge and wisdom, and represents the freedom our spiritual self seeks. It symbolizes the power that will unlock the Mysteries of the Ages and provide answers and solutions for our daily physical and spiritual lives.

The Dragonfly: In the physical world, the life of the dragonfly is short. In metaphysical symbolism, the dragonfly represents immortality and regeneration – birth, death, and birth again - which is the path of our own Spirit in human embodiment.

The Wings: The wings represent our real home, the Spirit world, and our ability to transcend all things. They also represent the all-pervading power and protection of the Creative Force (God), and the wings of protection wrapped around us.

The Orbs: The orb in the handle of the key represents the Central Sun, the center of the Universe, and the home and origin of God, or Infinite Intelligence. The smaller orb above and to the left represents Earth, and all things physical.

The Watch Movement: The movement represents change, and the need to overcome our fear of it. Each of the smaller sections of the movement represents the many aspects within each of us that must be individually transformed and transmuted so they might contribute to the unfoldment and progress of the whole self.

The Gear: The gear on the upper right symbolizes the artificial sense of time and mortality and the illusions of mankind, things that we must transcend in order to become aware of our individual place in the Cosmic Harmony of life.

Foreword

I cannot remember exactly when, how, or why I became fascinated by Natural Law. These laws could be referred to by a number of other names: Cosmic Law, Universal Law, or God's Laws are a few of the more common terms that many people use. They are the principles which govern how and why all of the Universe functions; and more importantly for the average person, they are tools which we can use to improve our daily lives. For students of metaphysics, and those in pursuit of developing and enhancing skills in mediumship in order to communicate with the Spirit World, the study of Natural Law is essential.

In the early 1980's, I heard about a place called Camp Chesterfield from a close friend whose mother had been there. We decided to take a road trip from Detroit – about a 4-hour journey - and do some exploration. We found a wonderful place, a 135-year-old Spiritualist center of esoteric and metaphysical teaching and demonstration, that immediately grabbed our interest. It is located about one hour north of Indianapolis, and one hour south of Ft. Wayne, Indiana in the town of Chesterfield, right off Interstate 69.

As I came to learn, Spiritualism is a spiritual philosophy of which guiding principles are a belief that we don't die. There is continuity of life after death, and we can communicate with those in the Spirit world. Spiritualism was a huge movement in the United States and in Europe from the 1870's well into the 1950's and 60's. At one time, there were hundreds of these types of *camps* similar to Chesterfield, across the United States. The three oldest, largest, and best known are Chesterfield, Lily Dale Assembly in New York state, and Cassadaga in Florida. There is also still a smattering of smaller camps left around the U.S.

On our next trip to Chesterfield, my friend Jim and I decided to take a few educational classes. It had gradually begun to dawn on me that 'my heart had come home', as I realized more and more that

Spiritualism offered what my soul was yearning. Among the three or four classes I initially chose was one on Natural Law. Spiritualists refer to these universal principles as *Natural Law*, as they are naturally occurring throughout the Cosmos as well as on Mother Earth. That class was taught by the Rev. Lois Mosteller, a resident medium, teacher, and later Board President there. Her lesson plan was drawn form a book by Raymond Holliwell called *Working With the Law*. From that class, my interest in and passion for Natural Law grew rapidly. My best guess is that it resonated with my Capricorn nature and logical mind, as it explained so much of the how and why of life, living, and our relationship to the Universal Life Force we call God. The more I read and studied, the more sense it made to me. Natural Law also explained spirit communication and the varied phenomena which are the heart and soul of Spiritualist teachings, by demonstrating that it all works based upon principles of science (meta-science or metaphysics).

What could possibly be better suited for a Capricorn than that? To have logic and science explain the mysterious without diminishing the mystical is the best of all worlds, in my humble opinion. And at a personal, day to day level, Natural Law helped me begin reflecting on past events in my life. Those reflections, seen through a new set of eyes and awakened consciousness, helped me achieve greater understanding. That new understanding helped me achieve healing on some old issues of mine. Later, I increasingly began to utilize Natural Law as a set of tools to become proactive and begin creating the conditions in my life, which I desired. The use of Natural Law as the way we achieve expansion of consciousness, remains an ongoing and unfolding process of self-discovery for each of us. Ultimately, it leads us to the personal power and potentiality that lies unrealized and untapped in each of us.

Besides life itself, Natural Law may be the greatest gift that God and Spirit could ever give us, for they are the true Keys to the Kingdom. As the saying goes, "God helps those who help themselves." Well, I have begun helping myself to the tool chest, while encouraging others to do the same. We are not powerless beings, and we don't have to remain that way, unless we choose to do so. Only those who truly do not have 'eyes to see and ears to hear' would ever allow themselves to remain powerless. Fully understanding Natural Law – let alone teaching it or writing about it – is a life-long process, yet central to the continuous unfolding of our souls over the eons. Though I have created extensive notes I draw upon when I teach this class, I realized that I have never taught this class the same way twice. Time and reflection continue to bring me new insights about the material I am using.

Often, I find that I am hearing a concept, example, or explanation for the first time as I am literally speaking the words while teaching a class. Nearly every time I find myself mentally saying, "Interesting. Where did that come from?" Of course, I now know the answer. It comes from the overshadowing and influence of Spirit. Sometimes, a question from one of my students will challenge me to explain something in a different way, which often results in my looking at things in a new manner that had not occurred to me before. I draw my material from many other sources: other teachers, various authors and books, a concept, a sentence or clip from a motion picture or television program, etc. In any case, I often adjust my notes to incorporate that new information and use it in future classes.

As to why I decided to attempt writing a book on Natural Law? Over the years many of my students kept asking me what (one) book they could obtain that would provide all the information needed. There wasn't one I could recommend. I finally decided to write one – at least one that was a good foundation for anyone to use. That was about ten years ago, and various parts of it sat unfinished until this year. Spirit kept prodding me in a variety of ways, but I think they had just about given up on me. Besides, it had never occurred to me to write any kind of book, let alone this one, so I had a lot of apprehension about it in the first place. I finally decided that 'things get done by doing them', and realized I had to start somewhere. I also decided that if I waited until I 'thought I had all the information there is' on Natural Law nothing would ever get put to paper. So, I started with the piles of notes I had accrued to teach the class and went from there. I want to be clear; this book does not presume to be all of the Natural Laws; but those first few impressed upon me by Spirit as the foundation for creation itself, especially as it relates to our taking charge of our lives. All the other Natural Laws? Well maybe we'll leave those for a second book.

~ Rev. Ryan

Acknowledgements

It is important that special thanks go to some of the people who have influenced me the most, not only in writing this book, but in my spiritual development as a medium and teacher, as well as over the course of my life.

First and foremost, I must thank my teacher, mentor, and friend, the Rev. Louise E. Irvine for setting me on the path of spiritual unfoldment, learning the true nature of Self, and my relationship to God and to other human beings. A resident staff medium and teacher at Camp Chesterfield, Louise held psychic development classes in her home nearly every weekend. I and my friends looked forward to making the trip down from Detroit to attend. These classes were designed to help new students interested in mediumship begin to develop the latent spiritual gifts that all people possess to a greater or lesser degree. But she didn't just teach psychic development by itself. She believed that mediums should have a strong foundation of integrity, ethics, and morality about their psychic work, and their resulting service to the general public. That foundation also applied to daily life and living, not just to the practice of mediumship. Her bottom line was, "never settle for less than the best you can achieve." Other than my parents and immediate family, she was one of the most important influences in my life. Louise was a tough, principled, caring, patient, kind, and wise teacher, utterly determined to bring out the best in every person who had the courage to seek out her teachings, counsel, and guidance. I have, in many ways, patterned my work with my own students based on how she guided me and many others.

One of the unexpected pleasures that arose from spending time with Louise was discovering I could teach. In fact, I became a pretty good teacher and made space in my life for this new element. It had never occurred to me that I might actually enjoy teaching. My focus was on developing good mediumship. Had it not been for Louise, I might never had taken up teaching metaphysics.

One fine summer day, Louise beckoned me across the lawn to her porch. Without any advance discussion about whether I could also develop as a teacher she said, "You are going to teach Meditation during August Seminary in two weeks, so you'd better start getting prepared." I was shocked - Meditation? Ugh! Even though I already knew the importance of meditation in improving the quality of one's life and its role in developing mediumship, I could not believe it, especially as I was struggling to make meditation work for me. FYI, I am still struggling. But as my fellow students in her development class would tell you (many of whom are now accomplished resident teachers and mediums at Camp Chesterfield), one simply did not say *no* to Rev. Irvine. So that was that. But in her wisdom, and to my good fortune, teaching is now one of my great joys.

My lifelong best friend, Rev. James Hafer, is the anchor in my life. Other valued friends and fellow travelers on the spiritual road include Rev. Glenda Cadarette, my 'sister' on the path, Rev. Wahna Irvine, Rev. Lynda Richey, Rev. Jane DeVore, and Rev. Mardell Wilson. Other teachers, now in the Spirit world, who have been great influences for me are the Rev. A. Win Srogi, Rev. Rev. Shirley Srogi, Rev. Suzanne Greer, Rev. Patricia Kennedy, Rev. Austin D. Wallace, Rev. Bill English, and Rev. Gladis Strohme. Special memories are held for my friend Shara Sincock, a friend and co-worker in my early days in a retail career, for taking me to my first reading with a medium long ago in Grand Rapids, Michigan. Thanks also to Rev. Ann Lumsden and her husband Wes, who encouraged - even insisted - that I try psychometry at one of their Wednesday night development classes, giving me my first taste of mediumship.

Finally, love, kudos, and immense thanks and appreciation to the Spirit World: to the influence of the Ascended Master Hilarion, and to my own spirit guides, who signed on for the difficult task of aiding me over a long life of experiences. Life truly is a journey, and not a destination.

Table of Contents

"If you do not make yourself equal to God, you cannot apprehend God; for like is known by like. Leap clear of all that is corporeal and make yourself grown to a like expanse with that greatness which is beyond all measure. Rise above all time and become eternal; then you will apprehend God. Think that for you too, nothing is impossible. Deem that you are immortal, and that you are able to grasp all things in your thought, to know every craft and science, find home in the haunts of every living creature; make yourself higher than all heights and lower than all depths; bring together in yourself all opposites of quality, heat and cold, dryness and fluidity; think that you are everywhere at once, on land, at sea, in heaven; think that you are not yet born, that you are in the womb, that you are young, that you are old, that you have died, that you are in the world beyond the grave. Grasp in your thought all of this at once, at all times and in all places; all substances and qualities and magnitudes together; then you can apprehend God. But if you shut up your soul in your body, and abase yourself, and say "I know nothing, I can do nothing; I am afraid of earth and sea, I cannot mount to heaven; I know not what I was, nor what I shall be", then what have you to do with God?"

~ **Hermes Trismegistus, Corpus Hermeticum XI (ii)**

Chapter 1: Introduction to Natural Law

> **"No man is above the law, and no man is below it."**
>
> ~ President Theodore Roosevelt

President Roosevelt's comments at the time referred to civil law, but I feel they also aptly apply to what we call Natural Law. In the context of Natural Law, the statement quoted above extends not only to every man, woman, and child on the planet, but to all things in existence. It is important to grasp the idea that we exist now and have always existed under the influence of Natural Law, for all eternity. It affects, and has affected, every aspect of our lives, relationships, careers, and general living in this life, all past lives, and will affect all future lives. We cannot escape its power and effects. Therefore, I feel it is vital that we learn how it works in order to live our lives in harmony with these great forces as they move throughout the Universe. By living in harmony with the Natural Laws, we empower ourselves to live happier, healthier, and more fulfilling lives.

There are two Universal forces which enable all the laws to work: energy and vibration. Energy powers vibration, and vibration determines, describes, and defines the nature of all things in the Universe. Vibration will be discussed in greater detail in a later section.

Natural law is not an immense force that leaves us powerless and at the whim and will of an arbitrary and vengeful God, or of any other power. Quite the contrary. There are portions of Natural Law that we can directly influence, and by doing so use the tools – for that is what they are, tools to change our life conditions for the better. You can think of Natural Law, if you wish, as *God's Toolbox*. By learning to use the 'power' tools within, we really are activating the God force that lies within each of us.

What is Natural Law? You can just as easily call it Universal Law, God's Law, Cosmic Law, Universal Mind, Divine Law, Law of the Infinite, Laws of Nature, or similar things. You will find many of these names used in a variety of ancient and modern texts on occult and esoteric studies. You can feel free to use any name which resonates with you. Spiritualists call it Natural Law, as it is naturally occurring throughout the various planes and dimensions of the Universe.

There are different ways to define these laws, as well. Spiritualists have adopted the following definition:

"Natural Law is that which God set into motion to govern all that has been created. It is immutable and unchangeable. There is no known instance where God has set aside these Laws in response to human appeal, or for any other reason."

A simpler and more contemporary definition is:

"The sum total of God in manifestation and action."

We more commonly say that "God is everywhere and in everything," or "All That Is."

Over time, mankind has created sets of laws at the local, state, national, and now international levels in an effort to establish a safer, more ordered society for the benefit of everyone. So, too, is there order and structure in all aspects of the Universe that govern the various planes, dimensions, celestial bodies, and everything that exists. Natural Law not only controls that process, but also explains how and why. It establishes powers, functions, attributes, and phases throughout the various planes of the Cosmos, and of course our own daily lives as well.

Natural Law does not tell us how to live our lives; the Laws are strictly impartial and not judgmental, and in themselves, are neither good nor bad. They only describe and define the influence of the Laws and possible outcomes, no matter the choices we make about life and living.

The Laws comprise the foundation of the Universe and always provide opportunities to achieve the best and the highest for ourselves as divine and immortal souls striving for self-realization and expansion of consciousness through right thinking, right acting, and right living.

There are two important aspects for us to be conscious of:

1. Natural Law becomes the expression of both acceptable and unacceptable behaviors, depending on the choices we make.

2. They are the ways in which cause and effect phenomena are related.

Perhaps the most frequently asked question on earth is, "What is the purpose of my life?" I would suggest that our ultimate purpose is to become awakened, self-aware, self-realized, conscious of our true nature, and to become God-like. Everything else is secondary in importance. All aspects of our many lifetimes are merely efforts to fulfill those goals and achieve our destiny. Understanding Natural Law helps us learn that we can take control of our life, in every lifetime, on our path to discovering that the God Force truly lies within each one of us.

Every soul spends eons living in a mostly unconscious state, unaware of its own true nature as a divine and immortal spirit, and that choices and decisions always result in consequences, be they good or bad. In this stage, we are unaware of the workings of Natural Law or its influence in our lives. But at some point in our existence, each of us becomes conscious, or self-aware, and develops the capacity of mind and thought in order to make better choices.

This also becomes a time when we can develop self-empowerment and strive to make the best possible choices to elevate our own life and the lives of others.

The Spiritual Masters have shared these ten principles to aid us in our understanding of Natural Law:

1. These laws represent the Universal Truth as we know it to be at this time.

2. The laws apply to everyone and everything, and provide justice and fairness to all, here or hereafter.

3. One cannot live a life outside Natural Law, and any attempt to do so will result in chaos.

4. The laws are absolute and perfect.

5. The laws provide a sense of order and balance. It is an illusion that our lives are unpredictable or filled with chance encounters and occurrences.

6. The laws provide us with a way of overcoming negative outcomes.

7. When we live according to the laws, we help not only ourselves, but others too.

8. We live in a holographic universe, and the whole is contained in each small particle. The microcosm and the macrocosm are aspects of the same thing.

9. The laws remind us that we live simultaneously in more than one world. Even as we currently experience the physical dimension, we are also a part of and bound by the unseen planes and dimensions. We are spirit in an embodiment of flesh, with figuratively each 'foot' planted in two different worlds: the physical and spiritual.

10. The next frontier for evolution is of the mind and its potentiality.

The natural condition of the Universe is one of balance, harmony, and order. When a disharmony or imbalance occurs, the Universe will create corrective forces to restore balance. So too, balance, harmony, and order are the natural conditions for our lives. But when there is an imbalance or disharmony in our lives, Natural Law can provide an explanation of why, and a way that we can undertake to correct the situation.

Even the concepts of good and evil are subject to Natural Law. Think of *good* as anything which tends toward the positive, unity, harmony, and balance. That is the natural state of all things. *Evil* is anything that tends toward the negative, imbalance, chaos, disharmony and disunity, and things which divide, separate, or erect barriers.

The origins of Natural Law are lost in ancient history and other mysteries of the Universe. As mentioned in the quote preceding this chapter, the introduction of Natural Law is credited to Hermes Trismegistus. More than likely, he was one of the Great Spirit entities we refer to as Ascended Masters, sent to Earth to help with the advancement of mankind. Manly Hall, in his wonderful book *Twelve World Teachers*, says that Hermes Trismegistus was a great Egyptian teacher in his own right, and may have been a contemporary of Moses. Hermes is credited with founding and writing about many great arts and sciences, including alchemy, magic, astronomy, astrology, mathematics, and others.

Today, Hermetism, or Hermetic Philosophy has become synonymous with Metaphysics and New Age thought. Most of us are familiar with the term 'hermetically sealed', a technique based on ancient principles, and attributed to this individual. In ancient writings we have found what are known as the Seven Hermetic Principles, which constitute the foundation of Natural Law. Those principles are:

➢ Mind, or mentalism   ➢ Correspondence

- Vibration
- Cause and effect
- Polarity
- Gender
- Rhythm

Another way to view Natural Law is through the lens of what are called the Laws of Analogy. The Ancient Axiom states in Latin, "ex uno disce omnes" or "by discovery of One, learn thou of All." One of the Laws of Analogy is the Hermetic Axiom, which we now call the Law of Correspondence. It states, "as above, so below." As you dig deeper into the material provided in this book, you will more thoroughly understand the meanings and applications of these Laws of Analogy.

There are many Natural Laws we know of, and likely many more that have not been revealed to us yet, as we may not be ready to understand them and their context in the structure of the Universe. In any event, this book will focus on the Nine Laws of the Cycles of Life. They are the Natural Laws which describe the process of creation, manifestation, and the outcomes that result from the creative process. Natural Law gives us the power and the mechanism to take charge of our lives, to live proactively and not reactively, and to create the conditions we desire in our lives, even as we live them.

Finally, one does not have to adhere to a particular faith, religion, practice, or belief to study Natural Law. No special training is required in advance, either. As we should do with all things, approach this material with an open and inquiring mind. I hope you will use these tools to empower your life.

Section I: The Laws of Creation

"Do you know what amazes me more than anything else? The impotence of force to organize anything. There are only two powers in the world: the Spirit and the sword. And in the long run, the sword will always be conquered by the Spirit."

~ Napoleon Bonaparte

Chapter 2: Introduction to Creation

The Laws of Creation are:

❖ The Law of Love (Wisdom)

❖ The Law of Mind (Will)

❖ The Law of Thought & Intention (Active Intelligence)

The Laws of Creation are one of the ways to describe what is called the *3-Fold Self*, which is referred to in many ancient and modern writings. The laws also represent an esoteric view of the Trinity referenced in Christian tradition. Taken together, they comprise the sublime essence of the God Force or Cosmic Consciousness. The Laws of Creation are the great constructive forces which flow throughout the Universe and are the causes by which all things have been created.

In considering the nature of these laws, we may initially be drawn to think of things in universal terms. However, their real importance to us, and the purpose of this book, lies in realizing that these three laws and the principle of creation they represent are the ways in which we can begin to change our lives for the better, at every level of our existence.

First though, it is time to consider the possibility of new realities that can significantly impact our self-awareness and assist us in absorbing and better understanding the Natural Laws and the materials contained within this book. One of those realities is that there is only one continuum in the Universe in which we exist, and the notion of one lifetime, 'one and done', is an illusion. Our real home is the Spirit world, and we come to the earth plane in as many lifetimes as we may need to learn and to expand our consciousness. In a sense, we have taken a view of our lives in kind of a one dimensional approach, i.e., looking at birth and death as a beginning and an ending. But birth is really an entryway, a portal, into physical expression, while death is merely the exit from this world. When a person can begin to wrap their minds around this idea, the fear of death begins to fade from our thoughts. More importantly, broadening one's horizon of thoughts helps explore the larger picture of life and existence.

It also is at this stage that we must begin to give serious thought to understanding who we really are, and what our relationship is to the God Force, to Infinite Intelligence, and to all other things in the Universe. Each of us is a divine and immortal spirit, an individualized spark of the God Force sent forth into the Universe in the Beginning. In ancient Greece, there was a sacred place called the Oracle of Delphi. Kings, scholars, sages, and paupers went to the Temple to consult the Oracle about many things. One of the most famous quotes spoken by the Oracle said, "Know Thyself, and Thou shalt know God." This quotation is also an expression of two central principles in metaphysics: as above, so below, and the macrocosm and the microcosm. If we could come to truly knowing and acknowledging every portion of WHO WE REALLY ARE, we would then understand that the God Force lies within each of us, awaiting our discovery and our self-actualization of all that we can become.

As a part of the God Force, we contain the same powers, attributes, and abilities as Active Intelligence itself. Many, if not most of those powers, are unrecognized and unrealized, hidden deep within us, awaiting sufficient expansion of consciousness to access and use them. One of those powers is the ability to create. Without realizing it, we are creating all the time, mostly in an unconscious manner. Fortunately, the thousands of thought-forms we create have a life span of seconds, and do not manifest.

In a sense, we have been asleep and unaware of our real nature. Over much time, many have progressed to the point where they can awaken and become self-aware while still in physical embodiment. Those individuals can begin to take charge of their physical lives and begin to create consciously and proactively, thinking, speaking, and making better and more positive choices leading to better life outcomes.

We should also look around the world and see the wondrous things mankind has created and bask in a sense of accomplishment from both our individual and collective efforts. But as we look around at what we have created, we must also see that we have created war, poverty, drug and alcohol addiction, suffering, hunger, homelessness, discrimination, and all the ills the world reveals. Issues of this kind cannot be rectified until a sufficient number of people can acknowledge what we have created and develop the will to take positive action. Waking up to who we really are will mean that, in the process of creating a better life for ourselves, we can also contribute to making a better world for all.

Each individual has been given the divine gift of free will and personal responsibility. The energies expressed through the Laws of Creation know neither good nor bad. It is how they are expressed and with what intent which determines the nature of what is created. Intention is everything. Our intentions should be clear, positive, and infused with love.

One important note about the Laws of Creation: they are the only part of the Laws of Nine over which we have any direct power or control. The Laws of Creation direct the functioning of all the other laws expressed in this book, and depend on whatever application of love, integrity, ethics, morality, and personal truth (or not) that we apply to them. Strive always to think, speak, and act in and for the best and the highest.

Finally, look at the chart below to have a better understanding of the relationship of these three laws and the direction of the energy which is generated when the laws are activated within our divine consciousness. This kind of chart is clearly one dimensional, and therefore limited in expressing the place, power, and scope these laws hold in the Universe. But it does provide a semblance of understanding. If you can get a basic grasp of the Laws of Creation, you are beginning to achieve how you can change your life.

The Creating Force

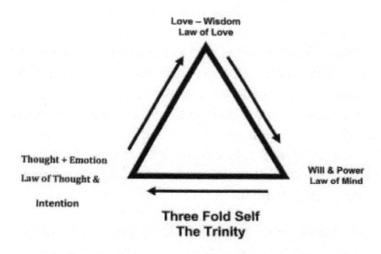

Love – Wisdom
Law of Love

Thought + Emotion
Law of Thought &
Intention

Will & Power
Law of Mind

**Three Fold Self
The Trinity**

Chapter 3: Law of Love

> **"God is love, and love is God expressed."**
>
> ~ Anonymous

Chapter Key Aspects:

- ✓ Love is the Creative Source and motivating power of all life.

- ✓ Love is purifying and lifts the heart and soul to the highest spiritual awareness.

- ✓ The highest levels of consciousness can only be reached through expressions of love.

- ✓ Love is the constructive force of all the other forces, and the highest vibration we currently know.

Some sacred texts refer to the Law of Love as the First Principle, or the First Cause. It is also referred to as the Love/Wisdom aspect when studying its relationship to other natural laws. Interestingly, this law proposes that true wisdom cannot be obtained unless we come from a place of love first in all our thoughts, words, and actions. The role of the wisdom aspect of love will be discussed in the next chapter on the Law of Mind.

This law has the potential to provide us with freedom from negativity, jealousy, hate, resentment, revenge, and other thoughts and feelings not in our best interest. Love also provides the potential for happiness, joy, abundance, fulfillment, and other positive qualities that can lead to achieving our greatest personal levels of well-being.

In order to grasp and use the tools of Natural Law, we must begin to come from, and through, the principle of love in all that we are and all that we do. Otherwise, the power of the other laws cannot be fully accessed or implemented. The truth of this statement is nowhere better expressed than a passage from the Bible, where great wisdom is often hidden in plain sight. The first portion of this passage is from Matthew Chapter 22: verses 37-40, and may be among the most widely quoted passages in the Bible, often familiar to non-Christians as well:

"Thou shalt love the Lord thy God with all thy heart, and with all thy soul, and with all thy mind, and thou shalt love thy neighbor as thyself."

The second portion of the text is rarely quoted, and even less understood, but equally important:

"On these two commandments hang all the laws."

This passage is essentially saying that the entire structure, applications, and use of all the natural laws, is dependent on what we do with the Law of Love.

The Law of Love has two key aspects: love of self, and love of all others and all things. At the core essence of this law, both aspects must be fulfilled as they are complimentary to one another; otherwise, the power of the law cannot be fully activated, and other laws become more difficult to implement. For example, we cannot really recognize the God principle within ourselves without also recognizing that principle in all others and all things, and vice versa.

It can be a challenge learning to truly love ourselves. Periodic self-evaluation is known to be a key component for those on the *Path of Enlightenment*. However, it often results in some self-criticism, embarrassment, loathing, even self-hatred. When that occurs, we are failing to apply the self-love aspect of this law. Needed improvements in our *Self* must be identified and reviewed with love, for that will allow us to proceed positively in making the necessary changes and corrections. Learning how to live life to the fullest should not be as difficult as we often make it. As Maxwell Maltz, a surgeon and writer says, "low self-esteem is like driving through life with your handbrake on."

To a greater or lesser degree, most people also probably struggle with what we call *Universal Love* or loving everyone and everything. Love comes in many forms. We can have a difficult time differentiating feelings of personal love in our relationships from that of loving everyone and everything else. Russian novelist Feodor Dostoevsky says, "Love a man even in his sin, for that love is a likeness of the divine love and is the summit of love on earth."

A key tenant of the Law of Love is worth a constant reminder as we go through our daily lives. This law is fully and completely without judgment or conditions. Period! This tenant is one of the most important messages that the Master Jesus gave us when he said, "love one another." This is a tenant that other great masters and teachers have also expressed. If we can work on self-love and Universal Love by adopting an attitude of non-judgment in all matters, we can more rapidly fulfill the power and mastery of this law. And it is important to remember every person – every soul – is always where they need to be, doing what it is they need to do, and doing the very best they can with their current state of consciousness. It doesn't mean we have to 'give them a pass' when they need to be held accountable – that is part of their journey too – but it does mean taking our own judgement and assessment out of it, for we are all doing the best we can do, too.

There is a wonderful quotation from an ancient text called the Mirdad. It says:

"You love that you may learn to live; you live that you may learn to love. No other lesson is required of you."

If we are fully loving ourselves, all others, and all things, then everything else will fall into place, and we become aligned and in harmony with all universal energies.

Throughout the ages, the Law of Love has been expressed in various forms in the writings of various lands, religions, and cultures. Demonstrating the universality of this principle:

Buddhist: One should seek for others the happiness one desires for himself.

Chinese: What one would not wish done to himself, do not unto others.

Christian: Do unto others what you would have them do unto you.

Egyptian: He sought for others the good he sought for himself; let him pass it on.

Hebrew: Whatsoever you do not wish your neighbor to do unto you, do not unto him.

Islam: Let none of you treat his brother in a way he himself would dislike being treated.

Persian: Do as you would be done by.

Roman: The law imprinted on the hearts of all men is to love members of society as themselves.

This law, as shown here with its universality across cultures and religions around the world, proves we are all working toward the same goals. It reminds us that every individual is on a path of spiritual unfoldment, albeit at different levels. It is love, not war, hate, or judgement that is the key to greater personal happiness and a better world. Non-judgement helps us be unified by the things we have and believe in common, and not divided by the things that make us different.

Applying this Law to Improve Your Life

> Review and refine the attitude and demeanor you present to others every day.

> Start small: a smile, a word of *hello* or other greeting to everyone will build into larger energies and efforts.

> Make a list of all the things that are right, great, perfect, positive about yourself. If you can't think of many or any, ask people you are closest to. Focusing more on your positive qualities will diminish your focus on (what you perceive to be) your negative aspects.

> When you are doing some introspection and self-evaluation, do so without judgement. Make the corrections you may identify and make them part of the 'new you'.

> **"There is a great man who makes every man feel small. But the really great man is the man who makes *every* man feel really great."** ~ G.K. Chesterton

Personally, I have a deep experience with the Law of Love. I am a Capricorn and have always tended to be somewhat Stoic about things. As I loosened up a bit in life – primarily due to my spiritual and metaphysical studies – I learned to describe myself to others as over-balanced mentally, and under-balanced emotionally; meaning that I usually intellectualized most things without feeling much about them at all. To others, I appeared serious a lot of the time. People began saying to me, "Why are you so serious? You need to smile more." For the longest time I blew off those comments. Finally, however, I began to think about it more, especially when I became interested in dating. Then in a class one day, I heard the teacher talk about first impressions. Every day, with every person, we are creating first impressions of ourselves all over again – even with people we have known a long time. The teacher's point was, "What is it that you want people to see, feel, and know about you in that first impression?"

So, other people's first impressions of me had been as a serious, non-smiling individual. I decided I wasn't happy with that, and I wanted to replace the serious face with one that had a smile on it most of the time. Like most things, that is habit we have learned, and to change a long standing habit isn't easy or quick. One of the tools I used was to practice random acts of kindness. Every store clerk, every waiter, every person I encountered was met first with a smile, and then a friendly comment. I quickly discovered how positively people reacted to that approach, and how much joy it brought them to have someone treat them kindly. Additionally, it brought me a kind of joy I had rarely known before too. This is just one small example of beginning to express universal love more frequently. Such joys also began to help me reduce my imbalance between intellect and emotions. I always cared about people, and the things that happened to them, but now I was allowing myself to also feel my care and concern. I also became able to begin consciously and willingly exploring the depths of Self – what I thought and felt about things, and why – and more and more I was glad to find things to work on in the way of self-improvement. Non- judgement is the essential key. It does not fall to us to judge others. Our only responsibility is to be honest, truthful, and loving with ourselves on the voyage of self-discovery and expansion of consciousness.

Chapter 4: Law of Mind

> **"Do not dwell in the past, do not dream of the future, but instead concentrate the mind on the present moment."**
>
> ~ Gautama Buddha

Chapter Key Aspects:

- ✓ The Universe is entirely mental in nature.

- ✓ Everything is connected to everything else.

- ✓ The higher mind has authority over the lower mind.

- ✓ What we think, say, and do affects all other things.

- ✓ A good state of mental balance provides the key to unlocking one's potential.

- ✓ True alignment of body, mind, emotions, and spirit is dependent upon one's mental balance.

This law is often referred to as the Law of Divine Oneness, meaning that all things originated with, and proceed from, the mind of God, or Creative Force. There are two central aspects: mind and emotion, or what we think and what we feel. Let us first examine the thought aspect.

Since everyone and everything has its origin with the God Force, then all things are connected to, and relate to, each other. Right thinking will lead to right speaking and acting, generating positive energies that result in positive outcomes for us and for all other people and things. The reverse is true as well. Flawed thinking will lead to negative consequences not only for the thinker, but everyone else too.

More often than not, we may think of our individual lives as separate and disconnected from anyone and anything else. While it is true that our life lessons are uniquely our own, we live and function as part of a larger unit, a greater whole. Larger issues – poverty, homelessness, the environment, etc. – do not hinge upon the thoughts, words, and decisions of one person, but rather upon the collective thinking, will, and desire of many people – the collective state of consciousness.

On the personal level, it is essential that we start by beginning to understand the nature of our own mind. There are two aspects of the principle of mind as it applies to the thinking process: the higher mind or higher consciousness, and the lower mind. The higher mind is a part of our Spirit self and connected to the Universal Consciousness, while the lower mind serves that portion of our physical self and is concerned and focused on the issues of daily life and living.

The principle is that the higher mind has authority and direction over the lower conscious mind, which is vital in the progression of each individual soul. For the most part, the lower mind does a wonderful job in managing all of our daily affairs. However, it operates much like a computer, and is dependent on the database at hand, acquired through all of our lifetimes of experiences, and through the five physical senses of our current lifetime.

Like a computer, however, the lower mind rejects anything that does not relate to its database. For example, the development of psychic and mediumistic skills is dependent on overcoming the automatic rejection of the lower mind, which does not recognize the aspects of our psychic/spiritual abilities, contacting and communicating with spirit entities, etc. Those aspects are experienced first through our higher mind and then, if at all, through the physical senses.

Our higher, divine mind is that part of us, which is never disconnected from the All, the God Source, the place within us where wisdom, vision, and true awareness exist. Over time, each individual soul progresses to a point where it becomes self- conscious, or self-aware, that it is not just a physical being, but a divine and immortal spirit temporarily inhabiting a body. This is a significant moment, for then that soul can begin learning to take conscious control of their current lifetime and become able to express free will while also understanding the need to accept personal responsibility for one's thoughts, words, and actions.

As growing awareness develops of what the higher mind has to offer, it begins to assert authority and direction over the lower mind. Often a struggle ensues, like a rider trying to break a wild horse. Gradually, the lower mind begins to become more subservient, more in attunement with the higher self. The result of that more harmonious alignment between higher and lower minds is better and clearer thinking and decision making. This, in turn, results in right-speaking and right-actions to ensure a happier and more fulfilling life for the individual, and also assists in creating a wiser, healthier, and more visionary society and world. It is at this point of awakening that the concept of expansion of consciousness also takes form in one's mind and becomes a desired objective that will propel the individual forward in its quest for greater wisdom.

It is vital that we work on bringing the lower mind into greater rapport, harmony, and attunement with our higher mind. Exercises such as meditation greatly help in this matter, for meditation requires the lower mind to learn to be still. When it starts to chatter less, we are able to experience, see, feel, and know higher states of consciousness. We literally begin to resonate with Divine Consciousness or Oneness, if even for a second or two. The small gaps of silence between thoughts in meditation are the places where we touch, however briefly, that Divine Oneness.

A comment about the word 'attunement'. The ancient concept was 'at-one-ment', or striving to align oneself with God, or the Universal Consciousness, and right thinking, speaking, and acting. Over time, it became the more modern attunement which speaks to vibrational harmony. *At-one-ment* was corrupted by the early church to *atonement*: to mean seeking forgiveness for one's sins, making peace with God, doing penance etc.

Achieving harmony between higher and lower mind, and then between body, mind, emotions, and spirit represents the path of unfoldment and the ability to maximize each life experience. Understanding this Law will illustrate the true meaning of equilibrium, or balance. Balance is meant to be our normal state of being. It is we who unbalance the situations and energies in our lives through unbalanced thoughts, which lead to words and actions reflecting that unbalanced state of mind. Actualizing the God Force within each of is only achieved through equilibrium.

Higher consciousness exists down to the subatomic level in all things. Everything is mind energy in the universe connected to everything else. This state of consciousness, or Divine Oneness, is a real force, or life force energy we often refer to as *prana*, or *chi*. The wonderful book *The Light Shall Set You Free*, refers to this energy force as the 'golden liquid light'. We can begin to access this energy and power by learning to train our lower mind to be in harmony and rapport with our higher consciousness and allow the vibrations of our higher mind to begin influencing our lives.

By using the power of the mind, man can create a mental flow of energy and direct his thoughts to manifest all that he desires. The mind is the governing power in the entire life of each person. Our condition in life is largely determined by our state of mind. As we improve and enlarge our mind, we improve and enlarge our lives. An old anonymous quotation says:

"In the final analysis, there is only mind. The only things of real value in the universe are ideas."

Everything is Divine Mind. The Universe exists within this field of energy and light. Everything has some level of consciousness: the planets and suns, animals, plants, rock, and all beings. As each of us begins to work on self, and empower our higher mind to guide our lives, all other things will fall into place. The principle of this law is that the mind is no greater than its conceptions. As we improve and enlarge our ideas and mental pictures, we will improve and enlarge our mind.

"Knowledge is knowing a tomato is a fruit. Wisdom is not putting it in a fruit salad." ~ Miles Kingston

---

Another vital aspect of the Law of Mind is the issue of will power. We cannot develop and utilize will power unless it first originates in our mind. Will power is essential to not only managing the tasks in our daily lives. It is also through the application of will that - as an immortal spirit - we can achieve change, growth, wisdom, expansion of consciousness, and spiritual progression. The application of will power in sufficient strength and force is the only way to accomplish our desired goals and objectives in any and every aspect of our life.

We do not tackle and complete a daily task until we decide that "We will it to be so." No project great or small is ever begun, let alone completed, without the 'will to do'. Will power is especially essential for people who may be addressing major issues, such as substance abuse, alcoholism, giving up smoking, dieting, etc. Once the mind is firmly set upon and determined about a particular issue and course of action, then sufficient will power can be created and directed for our use. *Strength of Will* is essential in the entire process of creation.

The exercise of free will – one of the greatest gifts given to us by God – is both a right and a huge responsibility. All aspects of will power, no matter how weak or how strong, are always manifested through the focal point of our free will. Through the trial-and-error system given to us, we make mistakes, and we make correct choices, learning when and how to make more of the latter as we achieve spiritual progression.

The *Principle of Dominant Desire* plays an important role in the expansion of our consciousness and the strengthening of our mind in ways necessary to achieve soul growth, and gain mastery in our daily lives. This principle says:

"All thoughts tend toward manifestation, but not all come to fruition, and the strongest intentions or desires in our mind will ultimately come into being, be it in this life, or a succeeding lifetime."

These dominant desires may also be unconscious in nature and may be impulses generated to fulfill karmic issues. These unconscious desires can also be positive or negative in nature and will, therefore, manifest themselves accordingly. The playing out of these dominant desires is a great part of our voyage of self-discovery to learn who we are and why we think and feel the way we do. As we become more self-aware, we develop greater discernment and ability to sort through all thoughts and desires and exercise our growing sense of free will and personal responsibility to make better and more appropriate choices and decisions.

Let's now take a look at the other aspect of Mind: that of emotion and the role that it plays. A quotation in the Bible found in Proverbs 7:23 says, "As he thinketh in his heart, so is he." This quotation at first seems confounding, as we know we do not 'think' in our hearts. But as we begin learning the role that the emotion process plays in Mind, it begins to make sense.

In, and of itself, thought would be one dimensional without incorporating emotion. Thought by itself is analytical and would lack important aspects in the decision-making process that only emotion can provide. We exist in a world that is built on duality. Emotion provides the counterbalance to thought. Making the right or the best decision results from considering both what we think and what we feel about something and requires us to strike the best balance or equilibrium we can achieve.

In deciding what decision to make about something, how often have we felt conflicted? Our mind (logic) tells us one thing, but our heart (emotion) tells us something else. Acknowledging both and striking the right balance between the two gives us the best opportunity to make the right decision. Sometimes that decision involves making a compromise, for the reality is that sometimes there is no *right* or *wrong* decision, only a series of choices from which to choose. Sometimes none of the available choices is particularly appealing, but that, too, is part of exercising free will and personal responsibility, and part of the growth of the soul. We can only do our very best.

So, what is the source, the origin of emotion? The Law of Love previously discussed is that source. The love aspect, once generated, infuses the thought/logic part of Mind, and becomes what we describe as emotion. The wisdom part of love contributes a vital ingredient to the thought process just as surely as the ingredients of water require both the hydrogen and oxygen atoms. That is why it is so vital that we do not dismiss emotion, and we consider it and include it in our thinking and decision-making process.

Nearly everyone at one time or another has met people who lean more heavily to the logic side or the emotional side. Those people who lean on just the facts as they see them to fuel their logic and decision-making almost entirely dismiss what they might feel about something. This is how they arrive at their rationale for having made the decisions or choices they did. Those people who lean heavily toward the emotional side tend not to give much if any consideration to the facts when they are presented with them. In fact, they can often create a (false) logic and rationale based on what they feel about something and use it as justification for their choices and decisions.

In both cases, balance and equilibrium are lacking, which can lead to flawed choices. Achieving the necessary balance is not necessarily easy, and more often than not, we do the best we can, and live with the consequences. This, too, is the art of the learning curve we all face to continue growing and gaining an expansion of our consciousness.

Applying this Law to Improve Your Life

> ➤ Think first before speaking or acting; what you firmly think you will realize.

> ➤ Never stop learning, studying, and growing; today's knowledge can be tomorrow's wisdom.

> ➤ The mind is like fertile ground; consider wisely what you wish to plant there.

> ➤ Give equal consideration to both our thoughts and our feelings.

"The state of your life is a direct reflection of the state of your mind and your thinking." ~ Author Unknown

---

My friend Mark was met with several personal life challenges over the years I knew him. He struggled with smoking, even though he knew smoking was bad. Later, alcohol and recreational drugs combined with smoking made for the Triple Crown of challenges that greatly impacting his life and happiness. Mark never seemed happy, but rather tried to get along the best he could at any given moment. His relationships were always unhappy and unsuccessful because he could not come to grips with the negative things hurting his life. At various times, Mark tried reducing or eliminating one of his three challenges, but always failed. He quit trying out of fear of failing yet again. His friends finally convinced him to get some counseling. One of his realizations that came out of counseling was low self-esteem, how little and how negatively he looked at himself.

Counseling helped him to learn how to start loving the person he saw in the mirror each morning. When he could do so on a regular basis, he began feeling more confident to tackle self-improvement by setting himself up for success instead of failure. Instead of trying to quit smoking cold turkey, he learned to first reduce smoking by gradually eliminating the number of cigarettes. Week one he smoked one less each day. Week two, he smoked two less each day, etc. When he realized he was making progress, his *will* to do even better kicked-in. Now, his strength of will became hungry for more success, and was so strong he would not even think about failing.

A willingness to learn to love the person he saw in the mirror, coupled with building on small successes, gave him the ability to access and develop his strength of will to succeed. Ultimately, Mark threw off all three of his demons, and he became the person he always wanted to be.

Fear of failure or seeming always to fail, cannot be allowed to find a spot for fertile growth within us. Life is eternal. We have all the time we will ever need to succeed and grow. We never, ever really fail; we just haven't succeeded yet.

Chapter 5: Law of Thought and Intention

> **"The thing always happens that you really believe in, and it is the firm belief in that thing."**
>
> ~ Frank Lloyd Wright, American Architect

Chapter Key Aspects:

- ✓ Thoughts are things; energy follows thought.

- ✓ What you choose, you create.

- ✓ What you energize, you will realize.

- ✓ Every change in condition must be preceded by a change in thinking.

Thought is one of the most powerful forces in the universe. In ongoing discussions of how the Universe was created, one idea is that the God Force 'thought' the Universe into existence. Like other natural laws, *Thought and Intention* is neither positive or negative in its nature; it is only in our application of the law that its quality and essence is defined. Intention is to have one's thoughts firmly fixed and concentrated on a goal, objective, or plan of action. Like the lens in a magnifying glass, intention becomes the focal point for the thoughts we are creating.

As the third of the *Laws of Creation*, one can consider the relationship of the three laws to each other in this fashion: Love/Wisdom is the initiating force; Mind/Willpower is the motivating force; and Thought/Intention is the creating force.

Before anything can come into manifestation, it must first be formed into thought.

In the Aquarian Gospel of Jesus, the Christ, there is one small passage which says, "Jesus taught his Disciples the Omnific Word, the Word of Power by which all the miracles were created." But even the Omnific Word must be created in thought before it can be spoken.

In one sense, thought is a subtle element. Yet it is an actual force in the Universe as real as electricity, light, heat, wind, nuclear power, or other forces. Thought is an unlimited force, and our power to think is inexhaustible. However, it has been said that we use only about 10% of our thinking capacity. Imagine our potential if we could use more of that power. Each person is constantly thinking almost every moment of every day; therefore, we are constantly creating too. What IS it we are thinking and creating?

We cannot stop thinking, but we can change our thoughts. Our goal every single day should be to direct our power of thinking into constructive expressions, always striving to do and be the best and the highest, and in doing so, give our thoughts the quality and essence we should always desire. When our thinking is unclear and unfocused, so is the energy that powers this law. When we change our thinking (including our attitudes), we can begin to change our lives for the better.

To better understand our thoughts and thought processes, we should consider the nature of thought forms. A thought form is a unique and individualized description of each and every thought we have with its own vibrational frequency. We have literally hundreds of thousands of thoughts/thought forms each day. Fortunately for us and for the world, nearly all thought forms have a life span of a few short seconds before they dissipate. However, when we continue to have the same thought over and over, the thought form gains mass and density. Ultimately, with considerable thought and focus and the accompanying strength of emotion, that thought form will be realized and come into manifestation.

Why? Because the law says, "thoughts are things, and energy follows thought." Whether we intended to or not, we directed energy to manifest that particular thought. If a thought form is positive in nature, then it will manifest a positive outcome. If negative in nature, it will manifest a negative outcome. People who live their daily lives with a bad attitude, a bad temper, a chip on their shoulder, gradually build a thought form or series of thought forms negative in nature that will eventually produce a pattern of negative outcomes. We all know people, sometimes whole families, that seem to have nothing but problems in their lives. That person or family group is constantly perpetuating the cycle of negativity. Every change in a condition must be preceded by a change in thinking; unless that happens, the cycle of negativity will continue.

The good news is that we have the power to manifest virtually anything we want! The more we think about something with clear focus and intent in the most positive way possible, we create a strong positive thought form that ultimately will manifest. Literally, 'heaven and earth' will move to bring it into manifestation because that is the law.

Individuals who set strong, clear goals and objectives for themselves, instituted by what is in their best interests and for their highest good, implemented by will power and self-discipline, will have their just rewards. There is a great quotation from the book *Working With the Law* by Raymond Holliwell. It says:

"You are the master of your circumstances; call forth your power, initiative and ingenuity, and be the master. Your fate is in your hands, so determine it."

There are four premises of how the mind and the thoughts it creates affects us:

1) The mind is the creative cause of all that transpires in our lives.

2) The personal conditions in our lives are the results of our actions.

3) All actions of man are the direct outcomes of his thoughts and ideas.

4) We never say or do anything until a thought has first been formed in our mind.

It is likely that almost all of us have had times in our lives where we faced a situation and found our mind telling us one thing (i.e., course of action or decision), and our feelings telling us something else. These are difficult times, but when we can achieve a harmonic balance between thought and emotion, we are then more likely to make the right decision.

Everything which we possess today, we created in our yesterdays. What we have tomorrow will largely be determined by the state of our mind and thinking and subsequent words and actions of today. Remember, where the attention goes, the energy flows. The best and most effective way to put this law to work on our behalf is to use both logic and feelings in creating our thoughts, and to then be clear about our intent.

People often seek private consultations from a medium or psychic, looking for guidance in their lives about career, relationships, and other matters. In many cases, they expect the medium or psychic to provide specific instructions or directions about what to do. If that happens, get up and get away. No person or Spirit can release you from the requirement that you must exercise your own free will and personal responsibility. Seeking guidance or clarity is one thing, and such consultations can indeed be helpful. When necessary, one can get professional guidance or seek out a neutral, non-judgmental person to hear our concerns. Spirit too, can and will, provide guidance to those in need who can hear them. But ultimately it is left to us to make a decision.

I urge every reader to consider these two key points:

- First, if you never remember anything else in this book, remember, "thoughts are things, and energy follows thought." That alone, when properly applied, will be immensely helpful.

- Second, remember, "every change in condition must be preceded by a change in thinking." Every condition or cycle remains what it is, until it is replaced by new conditions or cycles.

Remember the old saying, "if it hurts when you bang your head against the wall, stop doing that?" Likewise, if you seem unable to change a situation, stop and review your thoughts and attitudes about it. Changing those thoughts and attitudes can lead to a new approach or solution. The other old saying which applies here says, "if you keep on doing the same thing the same way, and expect different results, that is the first sign of insanity."

The Law of Thought and Intention is a powerful tool at our disposal; let's learn to use it accordingly in the best possible fashion.

Applying this Law to Improve Your Life

- ➢ Strive for balance between mind and emotions; don't let either overwhelm you.

- ➢ Positive thinking will bring positive things into your life.

- ➢ Constant positive thinking helps reduce and eliminate fears of all kinds.

Be smart on how this law can work for you. If you have spent most of this life creating difficult situations for yourself, suddenly transforming self into positive, clear-thinking will not immediately correct or get you out of your problems. It took time to create what you have now, and it may (or may not) take time for your change in thinking and attitude to bring about corrective actions from the Universe. Permanent, positive overall changes in thought, intention and attitude will set the tone for the rest of this lifetime and result in a better life.

If you are able to enlarge your mind enough to even consider the possibility that we all get more than one lifetime, it can help shift a bit away from the self-limiting thought that this life is all there is. You will find though, that you don't revert to thinking, "oh well, I have other lifetimes, so I don't need to work on this now." It does gradually become very freeing and helps us think and live better. As a friend recently reminded me, be kind to yourself, and know that you are doing the best you can.

Personal reflection space. How has this law impacted your life in the past and what future changes will you make?

Chapter 6: Section I Summary

Section One should now provide you with a general understanding of how all things are created. It should also begin to give you insights into three important things:

❖ That YOU have the power to create.

❖ A dawning realization of what you might have created in your past (and past lives) that has caused you to be where you are in your present life right now.

❖ That you have the power NOW to create, affect, define, shape, and then experience what it is you desire in the next moment, hour, day, year, and lifetime.

Each of us is responsible for where we are and where we want to be in life. Even those things which could be considered *karma* working-out in our life, are the result of thoughts, words, and actions we created at some prior point. Our decisions and choices – conscious or unconscious – have created our current reality. The problem is that throughout most of our existence we have been creating unconsciously. The results appear everywhere in our lives in the form of problems, obstacles, barriers, and living life reactively rather than proactively. Every time we think, speak, or act with little awareness of what we are thinking, saying, or doing, or why, we are *unconsciously* creating. It is only when we begin to become self-aware, and begin asking ourselves *WHY* we are thinking, feeling, and acting the way we do, and making corrections as we identify things that we no longer wish to be part of us, that we start being aware and start *conscious* creation through forethought before we speak or act. Then, each of us can begin to create the tomorrows we desire.

At this time, you may be wondering how you will remember everything we discussed in Section One. Remembering is not necessary. There is a difference between trying to remember and knowing and being conscious of something. As you give more and more thought and consideration to the ramifications – past, present, and future – of the Laws of Creation and how they work, you will gradually assimilate the information into that *knowing*. Then, it becomes a part of your being-ness in a way which will positively affect future thoughts and decisions, and help you create a better and happier life!

Remember free will and personal responsibility? We must always be willing to 'own' our decisions. The responsibility for what we have chosen to create cannot, and does not, belong to anyone else!

The paradox is that, in itself, the power of creation is an unlimited force, but always limited in its scope by our current state of consciousness. However, the infusion of love into the strength of your will, combined with clear and conscious thought and intent about what you desire, will activate the power of creation, and begin to give you more control over your life. Always think, feel, speak, act, and desire only the best and the highest for yourself, and you cannot go wrong.

The Circle of Creativity

What you think, you create.
What you create, you become.
What you become, you express.
What you express, you experience.
What you experience, you are.
What you are, you think.

Remember *The Creating Force* chart from page 26? Now that we have discussed its components in these past chapters, you should have a better understanding of its inner connectivity. Remembering, because it is one dimensional, it does not convey its true power.

The Creating Force

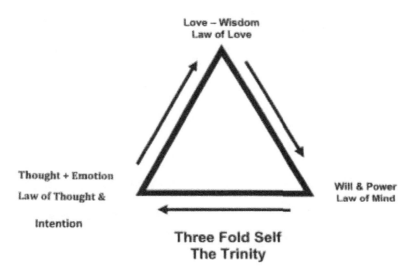

Love – Wisdom
Law of Love

Thought + Emotion
Law of Thought &
Intention

Will & Power
Law of Mind

Three Fold Self
The Trinity

Section II: The Laws of Manifestation

> *"Live a good life. If there are gods and they are just, then they will not care how devout you have been but will welcome you based on the virtues you have lived by. If there are gods but unjust, you should not want to worship them. If there are no gods, then you will be gone, but will have lived a noble life that will live on in the memories of your loved ones."*
>
> ~ Marcus Aurelius, Roman Emperor and Stoic Philosopher

Chapter 7: Introduction to Manifestation

The Laws of Manifestation are:

- ❖ The Law of Vibration

- ❖ The Law of Attraction

- ❖ The Law of Cause and Effect

The Three Laws of Manifestation are set into motion through what is initiated by the Laws of Creation. The clarity of our thoughts and intentions, infused with the love/wisdom aspect and powered by the strength of will, define and describe what it is which we wish to manifest. It is important to remember two things in this regard:

- First, lack of clarity in thought and intention, and/or lack of strength of will (reducing the strength of the thought forms we wish to create), or a lack of love/wisdom about the whole endeavor, often fail to provide Universal energy with sufficient direction to bring about the desired manifestation.

- Second, it cannot be said enough that we must remember energy is inherently neither good nor bad; it takes on the quality and essence of what we create with our mind. Negative thoughts create negative thought forms, and therefore negative outcomes. But the strength of our love, will, and thoughts and intentions – when always focused on the best and highest – will not only produce positive outcomes, but turn the tide of what might have been a long experience of negativity in one's life. Whatever has been defined and described by the creative laws, the manifesting laws will bring about accordingly.

The Law of Vibration plays an immensely important role, not only in Natural Law, but also in the Universe as a whole. The Law of Vibration determines and describes the entire nature of each thing. Our thoughts and feelings therefore determine and describe what vibrations will be set into motion. Those vibrations in turn determine what attractive forces are stimulated in the Law of Attraction. Then, the attractive forces, defined by the nature of their vibrations, will set into motion the corresponding causes, which can in turn bring about only those effects (results) that represent the essence and quality of the five preceding laws.

The following very basic example may provide an easier understanding of the relationships between the laws that are described above:

> Suppose in the house you have just purchased you do not like the color of the living room. You decide you would like to change the walls to be light blue in color and have them painted. Now, the beige carpeting and gold drapes no longer go with the blue walls, and they are changed accordingly to present a more harmonious appearance. Finally, you select new furniture which is complementary to the other elements of the room. You can think of the color blue as the Law of Vibration (determined by your thoughts and feelings for wanting to change the previous color), selecting new carpeting, drapes, and furniture as the Law of Attraction (you could only select colors and patterns which worked with the blue walls). Your dislike for the original color of the walls was the Cause, which results in the Effect of a completely re-decorated room.

The interactions of these six laws together will define how the aspects and workings of almost every other Natural Law play out in our individual lives and our world society, as a whole. The chart on the next page describes the relationship and movement of energy for the Laws of Manifestation. In particular, take note of the arrows on each chart throughout this book. Those arrows denote the movement and direction of the energy which is the motivating power for their activity. Compare this chart below with the one on page 55. You are looking at two out of the three components which comprise the Laws of Nine, one of the major cycles of completion in the Universe.

The Manifesting Force

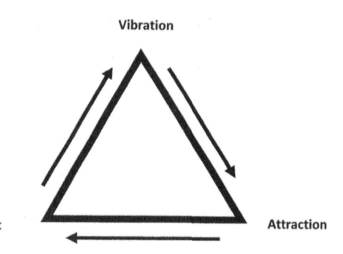

Vibration

Cause and Effect

Attraction

Chapter 8: Law of Vibration

"Look for the good in every person and every situation; you will almost always find it." ~ Brian Tracy

Chapter Key Aspects:

✓ Everything in the Universe vibrates, setting all things in motion.

✓ The individual rate of vibration of each thing determines and describes its nature.

✓ Everything vibrates at its natural frequency, and therefore is unique.

The Law of Vibration was known in ancient times as the Law of Power. Vibrations are the *fingerprints* of all things in the Universe. Since no two things in the Universe are truly identical, each thing has a unique and individualized vibration that represents the sum total of its nature and existence at any given point in time. This law applies in both the spiritual planes and in our physical world.

Psychic science teaches us that all matter is spiritual energy vibrating at different rates of frequency, and emanates from the Divine Mind, or Universal Life Force. The primary difference between matter and energy is in the rates of their vibrations.

Most people are more familiar with the word *frequency* than *vibration*. Frequency is defined as the number of periodic oscillations (or vibrations, or waves) per unit of time. We have seen hospital monitors used to track various aspects of a patient's condition, such as the heart rate. The monitor shows spikes and valleys in the frequency, the height and depth of the spikes, and the distance (length of time) between each spike. Health care workers have learned to interpret those patterns in order to better gauge the health and condition of a patient.

Generally speaking, the lower the vibration of a thing, the more-dense (or solid) it is, and vice versa. Thus, rocks, furniture, concrete, etc. have very low rates of vibration. Living organisms, such as trees and plants, animals, birds, etc. have still higher rates of vibration. Higher yet are the vibrations of humans. Above that, spiritual beings in all their forms and manifestations have increasingly higher vibrational rates. Heat, light, magnetism, electricity, color, sound, and other similar things have higher rates of vibration too.

The human ear can hear a certain range of vibrations, or pitches. Above or below that range, the ear cannot discern other sounds. Yet we know that animals and birds can hear (and sometimes feel) sounds or vibrations that we cannot. The human eye has its own limitations in what range of light and color it can perceive. Above and below that range of vibrations, we are unable to see other things and other colors.

In our daily living, we all understand and use our five physical senses: seeing, hearing, smelling, tasting, and feeling. Those five senses are aspects of our human self. All aspects of what is known as mediumship: the ability to see, hear, sense, and communicate with entities in the spirit world – are aspects of our spirit self. They vibrate at higher ranges than any of our physical senses.

To better understand how the rate of vibration determines the nature of a thing, consider ice. Ice is very dense – a lower vibration. But when heated, it becomes water. When still more heat is applied, it then becomes steam. When increased heat is applied, it becomes water vapor and no longer visible to the eye. Yet it is all composed of the same molecular structure, H_2O. All that has changed is the rate of vibration at each stage.

For those individuals who have had an aura photograph taken, you see examples of vibration or frequency. The auric field around us is electro-magnetic energy. Taken together, the various colors appearing in the aura are a snapshot in time, and represent the state of our mind, emotions, and health at that particular moment. Each color has its own unique vibration. The shade and depth of the color, its size and shape, and other factors can tell a trained auric field reader a lot about the physical, mental, and emotional state of an individual. A person whose aura photograph might show stress or physical exhaustion, could go get a relaxing massage, and return to get a second aura photograph taken. The color change and other factors can be quite dramatic, but all that has changed is that the massage caused relief from worry and stress, and relaxed the physical body (changing the mental, emotional, and physical vibrations of the individual), which, in turn, was reflected in a different color spectrum in the aura. It has been said that the aura of the master Jesus extended for several miles from his person, and people achieved healings by simply being touched by His aura. If so, those very high vibrations would be a direct reflection of the strength of His spirituality, state of consciousness, and personal unfoldment.

Our thoughts and emotions all have varying degrees of vibration which we radiate into the world around us. The collective thoughts and emotions of a group also have their own unique vibrations too. When one is assembling a prayer group, meditation, or psychic development group, the vibrations – state of mind, emotions, commitment, etc. – of each person should be considered carefully. The objective is to have a group of committed, like-minded people who then begin to generate a group vibration that is a synthesis of all the individuals. If the group continues in regular meetings with the same individuals attending, a harmonious group vibration can be generated that has tremendous power; producing healing and positive results for all who are participating.

Have you ever walked into a room full of people, and immediately felt uncomfortable, just as if someone punched you in the stomach? Or met someone new, and you immediately knew you 'didn't like their vibes'? Or, met someone new who you instantly liked, felt drawn to, and became best friends? If so, you experienced the Law of Vibration at work: the vibrational emanations, good or bad, of the other person, and how they affect and relate to your vibrations.

Each of us already belongs to a variety of groups: family, friends, co-workers, clubs, associations, political leaning, spiritual group, neighborhood, city, state, country; and of course, we are all part of the world community. Each group has its own unique vibrational signature, representing the collective consciousness and general thought trends of the individuals within that group. The state of our world reflects the current human community and its state of consciousness. Any group vibration or consciousness cannot and will not change until a change first occurs in a sufficient number of individuals. The issue of global warming and climate change, for example, and the required commitment to take preventive measures still hangs in the balance because not enough individuals have had a change in consciousness and embraced it as a great concern. Natural Law says:

"The energy that creates the solution must be at least equal to the energy that created the problem."

The study of *magic* is increasingly popular in this new Aquarian Age, especially as it seems to imply mysterious, mystical powers that one has or can assume through the proper training. The terms 'white magic' and 'black magic' are thrown around with little proper understanding of the meanings. Like everything else, magic is first and foremost energy, which we now understand is inherently neither good nor bad. So, white magic and black magic is entirely about the intent of the user, not the energy itself. The best definition of magic is, "the direction of energy in conformance with Will." Magic is thus Natural Law at work. True, magicians were and are individuals who have learned to consciously use natural law. The Master Jesus could be considered to be a magician. Any of us who choose to learn to use

66

conscious awareness in developing the use of natural law might be considered to be *magicians* too. Like all other things, the practice of magic is heavily dependent on the vibrational waves created. A spell requires that the words used are in relation to the proper intent, proper word, proper sequence, and proper intonation. This is important information for us on an everyday basis. As we begin consciously choosing *what* and *how* we say things, and what intonation is behind the words, we can make our own magic! Suppose you greet a store clerk with the words, "good morning." Your intonation is flat, and on top of that your face is somber. Compare that with a rousing, "Good morning!", and a smile on your face. You have just applied the principles of magic listed above and created an entirely new impression of yourself for the store clerk. You also probably feel better in the second example than in the first example.

Our personal growth, unfoldment, and transformation is always reflected in our rates of vibration. As we increasingly think, speak, and act more positively and lovingly toward everyone and everything, we increase – change – our rates of vibration to new, higher, and more positive frequencies; thus, reflecting our new state of thinking, feeling, being, and doing. It is only through our conscious desires and efforts to improve ourselves for the better that we can achieve continued personal transformation, unfoldment, and growth as a soul.

Applying this Law to Improve Your Life

> ➤ Think, speak, and act in the most positive ways possible, as often as possible.

> ➤ Avoid the influence and vibrations of negative people and circumstances whenever you can.

> ➤ Practice random acts of kindness, which will positively impact you in more ways than you might expect.

I believe all of us can look back to times in our lives that were filled with *magic*: an invigorating walk on the seashore during a warm and sunny day; genuine laughter and gratitude for a long delayed family reunion; the love and appreciation for family and friends who were there when you needed them most. Take a moment to reflect on that thought. Also, reflect on how many magical moments we purposely created. How many seemed to spontaneously happen? Begin to realize that we can create many more such moments as we willingly take charge of our lives!

Chapter 9: Law of Attraction

> **"Optimism is the quality more associated with attracting happiness and success than almost any other thing."**
>
> ~ Anonymous

Chapter Key Aspects:

- ✓ Like attracts like; things of like vibration tend to be attracted to one another.

- ✓ Attractive forces can be either positive or negative in their nature.

- ✓ The strength and intent of mind and willpower determines the nature of the attraction.

- ✓ Lines of attractive forces are always composed of the vibrations we have created with love, thought and intention.

The Law of Attraction operates along lines of electro-magnetic forces. There are two phases, or poles which form the basis of attraction: desire and expectation. Desire is the positive phase or pole. Expectation is the negative phase or pole (not negative in the sense of bad, but similar to electricity, with positive and negative poles).

Desire is the motive power that connects us with the thing we desire to manifest. It is the power for calling it forth into visible appearance or physical effect. Expectation is the force that actually draws it into our life. Here are some important aspects to consider:

- Never expect a thing you do not desire. When you do, you stimulate the negative pole or aspect that will surely manifest it.

- Never desire that which you do not expect to get. That is a waste of energy, as you are stimulating only the one pole.

- When we constantly expect that which you persistently desire, the lines of attractive forces become irresistible.

Let's look at a few simple examples:

> Supposing we are constantly worried that one fine day we will receive something in the mail we do not want: a letter from the IRS, an attorney's office, etc. We are constantly expecting something we do not desire, but are far more likely to get anyway, because expectation is what will draw it into our life.

> As another example, suppose we need another car to replace the one we have. The need for that car is constantly in our minds, while at the same time we continually say to ourselves we can't possibly afford it, so we know we are not going to get it. We are wasting time and energy worrying about it, as we don't expect to get it, negating that part of the law which would bring it to us.

The power of positive thinking, which is essentially the main theme of this law, is one of the most popular themes in self-help books. To truly work with the principles of this law, though, means we cannot just push out a positive thought about something we want and then sit back and wait for it to happen. We still have an active role to play in bringing things to fruition. So now is a good time to talk about an important set of principles which are true for all of the natural laws.

Most of us are familiar with two very common sayings: "let go, and let God" (take care of it) and "God helps those who help themselves." These two statements would seem to be in conflict with each other, but in fact they are not. Remember that the God force lies within each of us, making us co-creators with that great Universal force. As in the previous example, instead of saying, "I need a newer car, but I know I won't get one because (right now) there is no way to afford one," continue putting out the positive thought that you *need* the car, and you know you will find a way to make it happen. You also do the usual common sense things like checking on pricing, becoming clearer in what kind of vehicle will work best for you, leasing versus purchasing, etc. All the while you are doing that, momentum is building in the energy being generated around the whole process. In addition, I have found that Spirit can do the most amazing things in ways I could never dream of to accomplish something. Taking this approach means we are also flexing and using our free will and personal responsibility. Bottom line, using natural law requires our active participation. The laws really are *power tools*. But we would never pick up a chain saw, turn it on, and then not pay close attention to where we are directing it.

There is an old story I like about a man named Fred because it aptly illustrates the discussion above. It goes like this:

> Fred lived in a town near a river, in a comfortable two story house. In the fall, torrential rains developed, and flooding was imminent. The police department went door to door, urging residents to evacuate immediately. When Fred opened the door, he told the officer, "I've been praying to God, and he will save me." Soon, water came down the street, and quickly rose to waist height. Two men in a canoe came down the street and saw Fred. They yelled at him to get in and they would take him to safety. Once again, Fred replied, "I've been praying to God, and he will save me." The water climbed higher and higher, and Fred retreated to the second floor, watching the water out a bedroom window. A large motorboat came by, and the driver urged Fred to get in. A third time he replied, "I've been praying to God, and he will save me." When the water got so high, Fred retreated to the attic,

punched a hole in the ceiling, and climbed out on the roof. A helicopter flew overhead, letting down a rope ladder amide cries to Fred to climb on. A final time Fred replied, "I've been praying to God, and he will save me." Well, Fred drowned, and when he got to Heaven and stood before God he said, "God, didn't you hear my prayers, asking you to save me?" God replied, "I sent you a policeman, a canoe, a boat, and a helicopter. What more did you want me to do?"

We have created all the things in our individual lives, whether we want them or not, whether we feel they are good or bad for us, or even whether or not we can currently see what possible life lesson they could offer. Through diligent effort to understand the workings of natural law, and through a willingness and ability to examine and evaluate ourselves with love, we often can discover how and why people, situations, experiences, and challenges might have come into our lives.

The old adage "birds of a feather flock together" really is an expression of the Law of Attraction. Most of us can easily see why some people are in our lives: similar tastes, hobbies, interests, beliefs, etc. Other people, including life partners and intimate relationships, seem to be polar opposites of us with little or no common interests. Yet even those people are in our lives through lines of attraction. In these cases, the attractive forces may be karmic in nature in ways that will provide needed life lessons and personal growth.

The Law of Attraction is also the means by which our higher self draws to us our *Tests of Initiation*. These tests or challenges which may occur in our life are the means our higher self or higher consciousness uses to polish and refine areas within us that, in turn, will lead to greater unfoldment and spiritual progress. There is no one, and no thing, occurring in our lives that is accidental or a random, chance occurrence.

Applying this Law to Improve Your Life

> ➢ Living life daily with a positive attitude attracts positive people, situations, and events.

> ➢ Self-evaluation when made a part of everyday will help eliminate your negative thoughts, words, and actions.

> ➢ The power of positive thinking is an irresistible attracting force.

We should never desire what rightfully belongs to someone else. Rather, our desires should be directed at those things which will make our own lives fuller, happier, and healthier, and more joyful.

It is also important to note that many, many things can be created and drawn into our lives in this current lifetime. However, some things that occur in this lifetime were set in motion in a previous lifetime and are happening only because all the conditions for manifestation were not right before now. It is easy to forget that life is one continuum, divided up into what we call individual lifetimes only because we have been unaware before of the true nature of our existence as divine and immortal spirits. The more we can widen our field of view about unlimited possibility and potentiality, the greater permanent awareness we can develop as to the true nature of life and living, and the Universe.

Chapter 10: Law of Cause and Effect

> **"I believe that we are solely responsible for our choices, and that we have to accept the consequences of every deed, word and thought throughout our lifetime."**
>
> ~ Elisabeth Kubler-Ross

Chapter Key Aspects:

- ✓ There is no chance occurrence or coincidence; all is in Divine order.

- ✓ Every cause has its effect; every effect has its cause.

- ✓ All things happen in accordance with Natural Law.

In ancient times, this law was known as the law of retribution, for that seemed to be its usual result. Greater study of the law and its workings revealed that it, like all natural laws, is entirely neutral in terms of whether outcomes are positive or negative, good, or bad. The relative value or quality perceived in an outcome is often just the individual perspective of the beholder, as it has not yet revealed all the potential ramifications. An outcome that is initially perceived to be negative, for example, may in fact turn out to provide a valuable life lesson. This law also interacts very strongly with the law of karma and determines much of the kind of karma we create.

Each person is exercising free will each and every day through the choices and decisions we make, whether we realize it or not. Each day, as we think, speak, and act, we are setting into motion causes, which will always result in effects, desired or not. This law is another good reason to be consciously aware of what we are thinking, feeling, saying, and doing, for we are the ones who are creating all of the outcomes or consequences.

Take a look at all that you are and all that you have. You have created it all. In your review, you will find things you are happy about and thankful for, and likely also things you wish now hadn't occurred. Everything you see are the effects. Less easy to see or recall are what you did – or didn't do - that were the causes for it all. Remember too that the tone, shape, and definition of all the *effects* you see, were decided and set-in motion way back 'upstream', i.e., your thoughts emotions, words, and actions in the first three laws in Creation. Outcomes are merely the results of your prior work. The following example might best illustrate this discussion:

> Suppose you were at a restaurant or perhaps a friend's house and tried a new dish for the first time. You thought it was so fabulous that you got the recipe so you could make it at home. You assemble all the required ingredients, try to measure carefully, and follow the directions strictly. Finally, the dish is ready to taste. Upon tasting, however, it did not seem like the same dish you had first tried. The finished dish is the effect – the outcome – and the causes were all the steps you took in preparing the dish. Did you forget an ingredient, or read an instruction wrong, etc. that caused you to not achieve the right taste for this dish? Using Natural Law effectively is a skill set we learn to acquire over time – time which will inevitably involve some failed or not perfect tries. No matter: life is a journey and not a destination, and failing is important to how we ultimately achieve success.

Many people live their lives reacting or responding to events and outcomes, rather than consciously and proactively creating good thoughts that will produce good outcomes and consequences to improve their lives. Often this is the result of a lack of clarity and intention regarding life goals and objectives, and a lack of will power. Those individuals are more often experiencing the negative effects of this law, rather than experiencing the positive outcomes it can provide. Our positive thoughts and intentions create causes that will more often lead to positive effects, and the right results. While we cannot escape this law, we can influence its workings to benefit us. This can only be accomplished by clear thinking and intent, will, and personal discipline, to live and manifest a positive life.

This law, as with the other laws, operates on more than one plane at a time. The higher planes build mastery, while the lower planes complete unfinished business. Souls stay on the lower planes many lifetimes, until they have progressed sufficiently to begin releasing themselves from the pattern of creating more negative outcomes and consequences than positive ones. When we begin to reach higher states of consciousness, the Law of Cause and Effect (along with the Law of Attraction) helps bring us tests of initiation to strengthen the soul.

Sometimes, we can suddenly find an outcome or consequence which seems to appear in our life *out of nowhere*. Because there is only life eternal in one continuum, and because we live many lives, events experienced in the present may be the results of past life behaviors and actions (causes). The energies and situations that will allow the outcomes (effects) to manifest have not been right until now. Timing is everything in this law! Timing is right when all of the factors, conditions, and other energies are aligned to allow an effect to manifest.

When what we perceive to be unpleasant situations or challenges come into our lives, the occurrence may be for one of several reasons:

- Our current state of thinking and acting has resulted in unwanted effects.

- There is unfinished business (outcomes or effects) to be resolved or dealt with that could not have manifested until now because the conditions were not right.

- They are lessons that our soul must learn before we can advance our unfolding consciousness, spiritual progression, and enlightenment.

Applying this Law to Improve Your Life

➢ Become proactive rather than reactive; doing so will allow you to create outcomes you desire, rather than having to live with ones you don't.

➢ Change from solely experiencing what you created to creating what you wish to experience.

➢ Your life today is the effects of causes you created in your yesterdays. Today you are causing tomorrow's effects; do so wisely.

As you are reading this, stop right now for a moment. Where you are and what you are doing represents the 'now'. Yesterday is merely a memory, and tomorrow hasn't come yet, as you are creating tomorrow at this very moment. What do you want tomorrow to look like? What it will look like will be the effect of the causes you are creating each moment.

There was a time when we were all much younger souls and, much like our youth in this physical life, we were blissfully ignorant of many things. And like in our youth, we made a lot of mistakes, but that is how we learned. The system given to us for the growth and expansion of our consciousness is a trial-and-error system, whereby we learn why right thinking and decision making is good, and the alternative is bad. We need to experience both and learn the value of each to develop our discernment. Over many lifetimes and thousands of years, we probably created far more causes in our ignorance that kept bringing more negative effects than good ones. But since we are always the sum total of all our past lessons and experiences, we gradually began to learn the ropes of this thing called life and living. One of the greatest keys to success is self- awareness; knowing what we are about, and why.

Like any kid, when I was much younger I was always playing today, but looking forward to tomorrow, next week, next month, next year when I would be old enough to drive, etc. Most of us live that way to one degree or another. Doing so, however, takes away the full experience of today, of the now. It is not uncommon that when it really dawns on people that they are literally building their own life path forward – how wide, what kind of bricks or paving stones leading to where – that it seems overwhelming. While we might not often think about it, fully realizing we REALLY ARE in charge of ourselves is huge. It is a full-time job for all of us, some more than others. But rather than being overwhelmed at the thought, be invigorated instead, for nothing but possibility and potentiality lies ahead for those willing and able to take the wheel of their own life.

Personal reflection space. How has this law impacted your life in the past and what future changes will you make?

Chapter 11: Section II Summary

Several references were made that situations, events, challenges, or obstacles (effects) that appear in our current life – often with no obvious reasons we can readily identify – were set in motion (causes) in past lifetimes, and only now are manifesting because the conditions are right.

Only those people who are still 'asleep', meaning not conscious in this life that they are divine and immortal spirits, think in terms of living one lifetime that constitutes a beginning and an end. The purpose of every life is to provide opportunities to expand our consciousness and self-awareness, often defined as unfoldment, spiritual growth, or a number of other terms. An un-awakened civilization has created a thought system that looks at birth as a beginning and death as an ending. In actuality, birth and death are the two doorways we pass through departing from and returning to the Spirit world, our real home.

There is only one continuum of life, living, and existence. The multiple lifetimes on this planet (and perhaps others) are merely temporary stops along the way. Imagine if you were to buy a train or airline pass that, for an indefinite period of time, allowed you to travel from area to area of the country, stopping an infinite number of times at different places, staying each time long enough to get the full flavor of the place before you continued on? The journey counts as much – and sometimes more – than the destination.

That very simple example provides a larger view of existence and eternity. It is we who divide up the various stops into what we call lifetimes, but it is all one journey. The various laws of the Universe also transcend individual lifetimes, and thus provide the mechanism and the reason why it is possible to create causes in one lifetime –

through our thought and action patterns - that do not become the effects until a later lifetime.

We are always the sum total at any given point in time of all that we have previously learned and experienced – even if we cannot recall much or even most of it. (Being able to recall a lot of it could, in fact, impact or affect what we are to learn and experience in this lifetime). We have all seen or heard about *child prodigies* at ages five, six, seven, etc. who are virtuosos at the piano or violin, having received no training whatsoever. Where did those skill sets come from, if not from past life experiences? This example is just one of many that we could find.

Every day, we are building the path in front of us as we walk, stone by stone. What does our path look like, and where will it lead us? Conscious, thoughtful thinking and acting will begin to create causes and effects which bring us what we desire in this, and subsequent lifetimes, and we gradually slow the process of creating more karma for ourselves. We are Gods ourselves, so let's begin creating like a God.

A review of *The Manifesting Force* chart from page 61 represents the flow of energy we have initiated, and describes the process leading to manifestation of the focused thought forms we have created.

The Manifesting Force

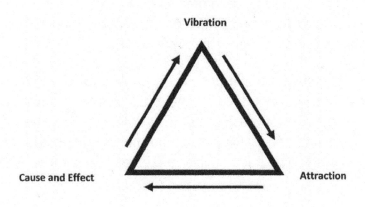

Section III: The Laws of Outcome

"To keep our face toward change and behave like free spirits in the presence of Fate, is strength undefeatable."

~ Helen Keller

Chapter 12: Introduction to Outcomes

The Laws of Outcomes are:

- ❖ The Law of Form and Substance

- ❖ The Law of Karma

- ❖ The Law of Progression

The laws in Section One and Two explain how everything is created and manifested. The laws in Section Three express and explain the final results, the outcome of the energies we have put into motion. An important commonality is that the laws in the three sections are Universal Laws over which we have a good deal of control or impact: some more than others. Those over which we have greatest control are the Laws of Creation. The Laws of Manifestation we have less direct control, as so much of these laws have been defined and set in motion by our efforts in Creation. These final Laws of Outcomes define how what we have created and manifested come into existence, and what the impacts might be.

If we have little or no control over Outcomes, you might ask why they should be of any importance to you? Every great (and not so great) artist started at the beginning of their career, perhaps learning first from others, but then over their body of work they define and refine their own skill set, like the use of color, drawings, texture, what mood they try to capture in the painting, etc. Every artist will have early creations they have thrown away, or not completed in their quest for greater expression. With time and practice, the artist becomes better and better at expressing on canvas – or in clay, metal, or another modality – the vision they have of it in their head – in their thoughts and emotions. Do we not also want to become more and more skilled creators in ways that benefit our lives and the lives of others?

Therefore, we should know how the Laws of Outcomes work so we can review our creative handiwork.

As young souls, mostly creating unconsciously, we created a lot of 'prototypes' that upon completion, inadequately expressed or totally got wrong what we thought we were creating. Without realizing it, over many lifetimes, we got better and better at creating and managing our lives, albeit still mostly creating unconsciously. Now that we have become self-conscious, self-aware, and have decided to proactively take charge of our life and expansion of consciousness, we can flex our creativity with new vision. By conscious and correct use of all the Laws, we can advance our spiritual progression while simultaneously improving and enriching our earth life.

The Laws of Outcomes represent major aspects of how our life unfolds and develops as we have exercised our power of free will for our highest good, if we chose to do so. If we didn't, then knowingly or not, we are allowing these laws to work out as they will; affected by other forces, energies, and events. For example, karma is being created on a daily basis. Did we choose what that karma will be? As our understanding about the workings of the various laws grows, we can more and more consciously choose to create the best possible future outcomes.

Life is really about spiritual progression and is the reason we are here in the first place. It has been said by the Masters that at any moment in time, no matter where we are and what we are doing, that is where we are supposed to be, doing what we are supposed to be doing. The purpose of life is to be – to exist, learn, grow, and expand our consciousness and understanding, and take the best lessons possible out of every moment, for it all contributes to our soul growth. So even if right now, at this very moment, what we are doing seems inconsequential, it still matters in the bigger picture.

At this point, you would have good reason to ask, "What about enjoyment? Can't we also enjoy life, our achievements, and the world? Does life always have to be a seemingly endless series of tasks and lessons?" Yes, enjoyment is always possible and achievable, and certainly desirable. And no, life is not always about tasks and lessons. The question always is, though, are we proactively and consciously creating our life (and therefore our future) minute by minute and day by day, or are we still living reactively to what we have previously created, or allowed others to create for us? Are we still allowing other people and events to have influence or even control over our lives? Periods of happiness, joy, prosperity, and fulfillment are the results of right thinking, speaking, and acting.

When the Soul Urge – that inner prompting for something more, something else - compels us to make changes, we will. I often refer to that Soul Urge as *Divine Discontent*. This is the path to mastery, whether it looks and feels like it or not. This is the same path the great Masters have walked before us. A profound quotation in the book *Conversations With God* by Neale Donald Walsh is where God says:

"I cannot know all that I AM, until I become all that I can BE."

As a spark of, and co-creators with the God-Force, that statement is a great description of the motivating force in our unquenchable desire to know more, be more, and be better!

Oftentimes in our lives, this expression and actualization is very much a struggle. Yet struggle itself is the result of a lack of clarity, understanding, direction, or insufficient experience. Hard as it might be to accept, struggle is a good thing, as it is the forge in which we are shaped and strengthened. Our struggles make the value of our future achievement even more important and worthwhile. The key lies in knowing this process is going on, while persevering throughout the challenges. Keep the faith! Remember you are greater than what and where you are right now.

This anonymous quotation aptly expresses the process:

"The day came when the desire to remain the same, was more painful than the urge to grow."

Take a look at *The Outcomes Force* chart below to follow the energy flow of the laws in this section.

The Outcomes Force

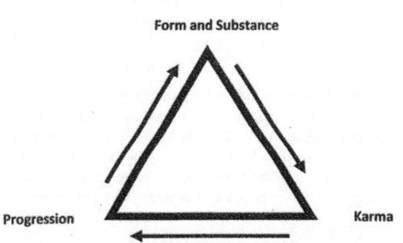

Chapter 13: Law of Form and Substance

Chapter Key Aspects:

- ✓ Form requires substance to be of value.

- ✓ Substance requires form in order to manifest.

Many wise people have often said that ideas are the only things of real value, for without them there would be no progress, no advancement of mankind. In considering this law, think of ideas as the substance, and the ways in which those ideas have come into manifestation as the forms. We have an unlimited number of examples upon which we could draw but here are a few simple ideas I use in my classes:

- Wine is the substance; the container is the form.

- A church building is the form, but the congregation is the substance.

Each requires the other to be of use and of value. Supposing there is a plentiful grape season, but more wine (substance) is made than there are containers (form) to bottle all of it. The excess wine may have to be poured out on the ground, as there are not enough containers to bring it all to market. Form is not adequate for all the substance. Or suppose a ten million dollar house is constructed, but the housing market crashes, no one ever occupies it. The house represents the form, and the occupants (would have) represented the substance.

Form and substance are not static qualities. All things in the Universe, from smallest to largest particle, are constantly in motion, and that motion creates change. Thus, form and substance are also changing - including the relationship between the two - even if we do not recognize it. Either the form has changed, and is no longer suitable to manifest the substance, or the substance has changed, and the current form no longer represents what is needed to manifest the substance. Let's say a church was built to hold three hundred people (form), but the congregation has grown to 800 people. The form is no longer adequate to manifest the substance. Either an addition has to be built, or an entirely new building must be maintained. One can have the greatest idea for a product (substance), but if no way is found to manufacture it (form), therefore the idea cannot yet come into manifestation.

Let's look at Leonardo da Vinci as an example. While he was known primarily for his great works of art, da Vinci was also a great inventor. Many sketches of his work have been found depicting plans for airplanes. Those sketches are the substance but, they were awaiting a way to bring them into form. Remember that da Vinci was praised and admired, but many people were also jealous of him, or hated him outright. I personally feel that da Vinci was – and is – a great master spirit whose primary job in that life was to inspire – not only the arts and culture, but to plant seeds of things for the future that people of that time had no ability to comprehend. I think that we could find many other examples of spirits who have always been part of an 'advance team' to whet people's curiosity.

Form and substance play integral roles in politics, government, religion, and all affairs of man. Suppose there is a growing spirit for freedom and democracy (substance) in a nation of oppressed people, and the current government is a dictatorship (form). The form is no longer adequate to meet the needs of the emerging substance, and revolution and war may occur to achieve a new and more suitable form.

Sometimes form and substance are mistaken for each other or are thought to be the same thing. A good example of the latter is that religion and spirituality are often thought to be – or promoted to be the same thing. But they are clearly not. Religion is the form, and spirituality is the substance. There are countless millions of people who faithfully attend church, temple, or synagogue, and are also very spiritual. But there are also at least an equal number of people who do not belong to any organized religion or faith tradition and have never set foot in a place of worship, who are themselves very spiritual individuals. Religion and spirituality can and do occur together, but they are still separate and distinct aspects.

The Laws of Creation and Manifestation play an important role. They provide the *DNA* of both form and substance and determine the initial nature of the relationship between the two. Again, what you have created and set loose flows *downhill* so to speak, and always represent the details of your creation, no matter how well or how poorly you have prepared the process.

Applying this Law to Improve Your Life

> ➤ Both form and substance require a creative mind. Let loose your imagination.

> ➤ If you achieve either form or substance, but are missing the other aspect, be patient; timing is everything.

> ➤ If you think you can or you think you can't, you're right.

If substance does not have potential form through which to manifest and express, then it will have to wait until conditions are right. In the example of da Vinci and the airplane, it took hundreds of years until the advent of the Wright Brothers and others before there was enough form to even construct a rudimentary aircraft. Sometimes we see form being constructed to specifically manifest a substance in a certain way. As I write this, one of the auto manufacturers announced they are building massive 3-D printers to make large car parts. So, in your creation phase, don't just daydream about an idea; also begin allowing your mind ways in which it can be brought into form.

Actually, we have no direct or indirect control over this law but can improve prospects for the best expression of this law by applying the Law of Change. As we have discussed, all things are in motion in the Universe, and that motion creates change. Everything has, is, and will continue to change. Our best move is to eliminate the fear of change. Instead, expect it, embrace it, look forward to it. Trying to remain the same is impossible, and the effort to do so becomes painful. A positive attitude about change can allow what you have created to manifest and express fully.

Personal reflection space. How has this law impacted your life in the past and what future changes will you make?

Chapter 14: Law of Karma

Chapter Key Aspects:

✓ Every action has its karmic reaction.

✓ We are free to choose our own actions.

✓ Karma can be considered good or bad, depending on what we create.

Not to be confused with Dharma (an aspect of truth or reality), Karma is:

"The sum and consequences of a person's actions during successive phases of his existence, regarded as determining his or her destiny."

The reference to successive phases of our existence refers to the many lifetimes we have spent and will spend in this and other worlds. There are two types of karma: mutable and immutable, or that which we can change and that which we cannot. Examples of immutable karma would be things like our current race or ethnicity, our ancestry, our gender. An example of mutable karma might be living in poverty in this and previous lifetimes. A kind of poverty consciousness may have been created by repeated lives where what we had and were given was wasted, spent unwisely, used frivolously, or squandered. The lessons needed – to use resources wisely, to save and give appropriately, etc. – were never learned, and so those lessons keep recurring in subsequent lifetimes. That condition will continue until the lessons are learned. Thankfully, once any lesson is truly learned and understood, it will not be repeated again.

There is no predictable pattern as to when and how a particular lesson will get worked out. The conditions must be right in order for a lesson to be presented, so we can work on resolving it. A karmic lesson that was created in the last lifetime will not necessarily be presented for resolution in this lifetime if the necessary conditions for the needed lesson and resolution are not present. It might take three more lifetimes, for example, before the conditions are right again to allow the lesson to be presented to us and learned, and for resolution to be achieved.

This is a key reason why someone can feel blindsided when a major lesson appears, and we thoroughly examine our life to see what we could possibly have done that would have brought this lesson now. The appearance of the lesson seems in a sense to be totally 'out of context'. To the unknowing, it can seem like the Universe has dealt us a cruel blow. But to those with a greater vision, it can become clear that some conditions must exist now that allowed the lesson created in past lifetimes ago to appear. There is only one continuum of immortal life; it is our limited perceptions which cause us to think that there is only one life, one opportunity to live and grow, and that then we are done.

Each of us has most likely carried some karmic debt into this lifetime; some of it may get worked out now, and some later. But it cannot be emphasized enough that we have 'all the time there is' to complete our lessons and can do so at our own speed and capacity, in order to understand the value of each lesson. Karmic debt is composed of:

- Experiences we will have that are lessons we did not have in prior lifetimes.

- A need to compensate for things we should not have done.

- Continuation of things left undone.

- New karma which we have created in this lifetime.

- The working out or fulfillment of agreements or contracts made with other souls, or with higher Guiding Forces.

In each lifetime we have a kind of karmic profile that consists of our knowledge, attitude, behavior, and beliefs, our talents, personality, preferences, goals, objectives, and many more things. This karmic profile is also a composite of both mutable and immutable karma. In most cases, we do not know in this lifetime the reasons for our karma. On rare occasions, some of us may have a flashback to another life or have a dream that gives us glimpses or partial answers.

Karma is the result or outcome of the decisions and choices we make, and the actions we take, within the framework of free will and personal responsibility. It is the highest form of justice, as it is self-regulated and self-administered. That is because we each create our own karma, not anyone else.

Whatever amount of energy we expend in our thoughts, words, and actions, a like amount is returned to us. The nature of the energy and form returned is greatly dependent on what we have created and put forth. In other words, where we are and what we have today is the direct result of our thoughts, words, and actions of our yesterdays. What will tomorrow be like? It is determined by today's choices and actions. For every action, there is a reaction, a result or outcome. Whether we will consider that outcome good or bad is dependent upon us.

It may be fair to say that the majority of people tend to think of negative or bad things at the very mention of the word karma. But karma, in and of itself, like all energy activity, is neither good nor bad, but merely a reflection of the quality of the actions that created it in the first place. The root meaning of the word Karma is *action*. We can work toward true freedom – freedom of self and from self. Freedom of self means freedom from neurotic based emotions such as jealousy, hate, greed, possessiveness, malice, resentment, etc. to name just a few, and freedom from all other negative thoughts and emotions.

Change begins with action. Creating more positive thoughts and taking more positive actions will lead to positive outcomes (creating *good* karma). And, as we start eliminating people and situations in our life that have contributed to our not only creating *bad* karma, but which have also helped perpetuate our karmic debts, we will begin taking control of our destiny in this and subsequent lifetimes. When we slow the creation of any more *bad* karma, we are beginning to assert our free will while also taking personal responsibility.

As we begin to understand more about how karma might be working in our life and the lives of others, we must avoid becoming judgmental. For example, consider the many people who are poor or living in poverty, based on the example given above. Would we decide to withhold a donation, or decide not to help someone because we now think we *understand* why they are poor? Doing so might only create karmic implications for us instead.

Karma is nowhere as simple as the information provided in these few pages. There are many connections and relationships between the various Laws, with sometimes an infinite amount of complexity as to how it all might work out in any given situation. Your heart and your mind, together with plain old fashioned common sense, should still guide your thoughts, words, actions, and decisions.

> **"The true value of a human being is determined primarily by the measure and the sense in which he has attained liberation from self."** ~ Albert Einstein

Applying this Law to Improve Your Life

> Strive to think, speak, and act from only the highest perspective.

> Practice forgiveness and unconditional love.

> Be kind and generous.

> We are fully responsible for everything we are, everything we have, and everything we will become.

Since most people are unaware what karma is, or the implications it may hold in their lives, they are unconsciously creating karma nearly every day. Your 'State of Consciousness' is the single most important determinant in where a person is and what they are doing at any given time. If we are self-aware, in the moment, and self-conscious, we are in a positive state of mind that will more and more help us create only the best for ourselves.

If you are consciously creating every day in your life, the good news is that you do not have to focus on what kind of karma you may be creating; it will take care of itself as you are working from the best and highest place consciously. We cannot 'work' on karma directly anyway. Instead, the solution lies in Section One and the Laws of Creation. By the time we get to thinking about karma, we have already created it. Simply striving to do the right thing every day takes care of shaping this and a multitude of other laws.

Personal reflection space. How has this law impacted your life in the past and what future changes will you make?

Chapter 15: Law of Progression

> "We shall not cease from exploration and in the end, all our exploring will be to arrive where we started, and to truly know the place for the first time." ~ T.S. Eliot

Chapter Key Aspects:

- ✓ Provides the assurance of constant evolution, progression, and unfoldment of all things, including the human spirit.

- ✓ Represents the accumulated knowledge, wisdom, and experience of all lifetimes to this point in time.

- ✓ Is the force which impels us to achieve, to excel, to know, to experience.

Each individual expression of the Creative Force – be it mineral, vegetable, animal, or human – is constantly striving to move to a higher state of consciousness and existence for itself. This striving is caused by two things:

- First, all things are composed of and originate from the Creative Force, and therefore contain some level of intelligence, consciousness, and awareness of its origin.
- Second, all things in the universe are constantly in motion; that motion creates change, which provides the necessary energy to power the impulse to seek something higher and better.

The Law of Progression is, in great part, the motivating force behind each person's desire to know and understand his or her purpose for being, and for the purpose of the present life at hand. It is the driving force to conquer a mountain, find a cure for cancer, run a marathon, or simply to improve one's mind, emotions, and current life experiences. Within the core or seed atoms of all things exists the absolute knowingness that 'there is something more, something better'. That knowingness and desire is expressed in the book *Conversations with God* by Neale Donald Walsh, when God says to the author, "I AM striving to become the next best, greatest version of who I really AM, and who I can become."

That idea is true for each of us, be it in this life, a previous life, or a subsequent lifetime. At the center of our Beingness lies the urge to know, be, express, and experience *all that I can be*. The heartbeat of Universal Consciousness in our center resonates with the awareness of 'I know there is more to who I AM' (than who I am now). That awareness comes from the God Force itself.

The New Year resolutions so many of us make each January also have their origin from our inner self, no matter how inconsequential they might seem. The inner sense of *I can do better, be better* is a strong impulse. It doesn't matter what the resolution is for, so long as it is positive in nature. Each resolution or desire for improvement will play its own role in our overall progression as a spirit. It also doesn't matter in the big picture if we seemingly *fail*. As long as it remains important to us, we will pick up that resolution again, in this or other lifetimes. Besides, failure as we perceive it to be does not exist in the first place. Instead, it is only that we have not yet achieved a goal or objective or *succeeded*.

Our progress and unfoldment is continuous; we grow and change even though it may not be readily apparent to us. The reason our growth may not be apparent to us at first is because of an ancient principle: 'as within, so without'. This is the same principle, 'as above, so below' differently applied. Meaning, we change first in our inner self on the inner planes - below our current awareness and consciousness - before we make outer, physical world changes. For example, remember when someone complimented you on something positive in your appearance, and you are, at first, startled because you had not realized it yet yourself? When that happens, they are often not referring to your apparel, but rather to the energy, the *glow*, the vibration you are giving off.

Most of us, even those individuals who believe that we experience many physical lifetimes, often unconsciously think of each life from birth to death as a cycle of completion and progression; it is. However, each of us experiences numerous cycles of completion within the same lifetime. We change relationships, jobs, places where we live, our attitudes, hobbies, and all manner of life activities. They all are part of the expression of the Law of Progression. Yet all momentum in these cycles is driven by the desire for something more, something better, something higher.

No matter what the challenge or the change required, it is all part of a vast pattern in the Universe. Strong, constant faith is important to see us through to the better times and conditions that will inevitably come to us if we will persevere. We, literally, have all the time in the Universe to get there.

Applying this Law to Improve Your Life

> Be patient. Be persistent.

> Never give up on yourself.

> Everything you seek is within your reach, if not your grasp; reach further.

> BELIEVE that you deserve better and can achieve it.

The text above has a couple of aspects. The Law of Progression viewed in the context of finally seeing what you set in motion in the Laws of Creation seems to indicate the end of the journey. Nine laws and their importance and interaction have been described, and that cycle is complete. You can use the Law of Progression to look back at the process from beginning to end. Doing so will help us get better at creating! This is where being self-aware is a huge help in the examination process. But the Law of Progression is also as described above: that constant desire to improve, change, grow, etc. The polarity in this law is both an ending and a beginning. As the nine laws are a completion at the microcosmic level, the urge to grow is a continuous force at the macrocosmic level. All things in the Universe are constantly changing in a never-ending cycle. When a cycle is completed, a new one begins again. And so, it is!

How many times has each of us been presented with a great opportunity, but turned it down? A big promotion but in a different city? A once in a lifetime trip to Africa that we miss because we are secretly scared to experience new cultures, food, etc.? Begin instead to consider WHY it is you wish to decline and look for alternate ways and means to say *YES* more often. Let the forces of curiosity and excitement sweep you away more often. Answer the call to climb that mountain! Choose better and more exciting tomorrows for yourself, and you will be amazed at how that changes your life.

Chapter 16: Section III Summary

All of the laws in Sections One and Two ultimately are expressed through our thoughts, which, in turn, determines the forms we create in our lives, any relevant substance we can derive, what karma if any we have created, good, bad, or indifferent, and finally the spiritual progression we may have achieved. At this point, the cycle of creation is complete for each thought form that has been given sufficient strength of will, and the focus of great intention to set the forces of manifestation to work. Hopefully, each and every thought has been infused with the highest qualities of love possible, so that 'downstream', where outcomes are determined, they will be for our greatest good.

It is important to realize that many, perhaps most, of our thought forms are *bundles* of smaller, more individualized thoughts. For example, someone who has an invention in mind has to consider many things: function, design, size, materials, etc. Every one of those considerations represents a specific thought form that, when combined with other related thought forms, is part of a bundle which, if executed properly, will result in say, a coffee maker. And, if any one of the individual thoughts is incomplete or incorrect, form and substance cannot align properly.

When we consider what Active Intelligence has created in the Universe, in our world, and around our daily lives, we cannot help but be awed by the power, imagination, majesty, and beauty we see, especially in the things we find in Nature. In our own way, in our own lives, we also are working hard to learn to create outcomes which have that same power, imagination, majesty, and beauty.

The Laws of Outcomes are where we can see our greatest visions materialize, or our worst fears appear, depending entirely on the quality of our thinking in the Laws of Creation. In particular, Free Will is a great determinant in what results we achieve. As we exercise that free will, we will make both good and bad decisions. However, trial and error are the governing system we have been given to use by higher Spiritual Powers. It is expected that we will make wrong choices as well as right ones; that is the way we learn the relative value of a thing, and how to make better choices more often. So, in the Laws of Outcomes we can see the results of our thoughts, words, and actions. Often, we see that different thinking, or a different approach is required, as the results did not meet our expectations. The Law of Progression is always fulfilled, even when we don't make any actual *progress* in a particular situation or endeavor.

Do not let yourself be dismayed if the outcomes are not what you expected or desired! Re-calibrate your thinking and begin again.

The Outcomes Force chart below, like the charts in the previous two sections, describes the flow of energy which produces outcomes in our lives. In this case however, the process has come to a culmination, a completion of the whole cycle. Since energy, in and of itself, cannot be destroyed – only changed in its nature, the energy in any particular cycle returns to the Source: God, Active Intelligence, etc. Since we are co-creators with the Source, the energy returns to us. There is an unlimited amount of energy in the Universe; it is merely our perception of lack, of a finite amount, that gets in our way. When we can eliminate that perception, we can move more fully into our creative abilities.

The Outcomes Force

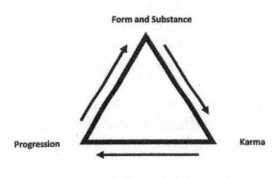

Form and Substance

Progression

Karma

110

Chapter 17: Afterthoughts to Natural Law

What we have covered in this book is how we create, what the manifestation process looks like, and what outcomes we have achieved. The triangle diagram in each section in itself can be viewed as representing the Three Fold Self, a core principle in metaphysical and occult studies. If one was to take all three of the triangles and paste them together, you would have a 3-dimensional three-sided pyramid called a tetrahedron, which can also be looked at as also representing the Three Fold Self. There are many laws and many ways in which the Three Fold Self can be described and expressed, appropriate as the nature of God is limitless.

If you've gotten this far in the book, you have been given a lot of information to consider, but don't be concerned about how you are going to remember it all; you do not need to. Much of the information will be more important to the metaphysical student than to the casual reader, as those individuals have taken on the life-long process of exploring the Universe in depth. They need to know the interactions of the various laws, and how to apply them. For everyone, remember these two points:

- First, we all are a part of the God Force, and as such are immortal, and co-creators with God.

- Second, we have been given free will, and must develop personal responsibility, knowing that our fate is in our own hands.

For the Nine Laws, I will outline in the simplest terms possible the three most important things to remember:

➢ Always strive to live, be, radiate positive thinking and a positive attitude in all situations. If you do this, you are automatically 'seeding' the quality of all your thoughts, and all that comes after.

> Thoughts are things, and energy follows thought. Remembering that as many times daily as necessary is vital, as we are constantly creating, and need to know what we are creating.

> Every change in condition requires first a change in thinking. Or you can say it as, to change something, change your thinking first.

That is all you have to remember. If you are manifesting those aspects daily, everything below in the rest of the Nine Laws is being shaped accordingly and automatically. These simple tips can empower you right now to start changing your life for the better. Remember to first have clear thinking about what that new life would look like.

I want to reiterate that nothing happens in the Universe that is unrelated to anything else. The working of the Nine Laws does not occur in a vacuum, and in actuality, could not function that way. That means even the Laws of Creation, one of our highest and most direct interactions with the God Force, is ultimately tied to, and even dependent upon, the workings of other vibratory forces great and small. In our human expression, we often say *timing is everything*, or *the timing isn't right yet*. Time has nothing to do with it, as there is no time in the Universe. What actually may be said instead is: *the vibrations are not fully aligned yet*. Many of those vibrations may be unknown to us in any way, shape, or form. No matter: our focus should always be upon what is within our right and our ability to affect.

As of this writing, our country is being slammed by a pandemic. We have had four years of political turmoil coming to a conclusion. We are trying to avoid an economic meltdown and assist millions of people in need. Social justice came to the fore, in the form of *Black Lives Matter*. To top it off, we are dealing with calamitous weather and environmental issues in the form of disastrous fires in the West, and hurricanes in the South. All these scenarios are different from each other, so it is easy to say that we really have had a string of bad luck. What are the odds of them all happening at the same time? A coincidence?

There are far higher and greater vibrations and activities happening in the spiritual realms that represent agents of change at massive levels in the Universe. They tie what I have described together in ways we cannot possibly begin to imagine; even if we could, we might not understand why.

The average person will look at only the things that directly affect them right now, and in essence look at them through a kind of tunnel vision. If one is able, more and more, to step back to see the larger picture and the greater context of what is going on, it tends to bring a greater sense of peace and calm. I am not proposing you are going to understand how and why things are connected to each other. But just the willingness to even accept there might be other dynamics at work will help you more easily keep calm in trying times. Realize too, if you can, that you are important, what you are doing and where is important, and that your life matters. In the microcosm, each of us is the living, breathing, walking, talking manifestation of the God Force, so how can you be unimportant? Likely you have never thought or described yourself in that way. Maybe trying to do so feels uncomfortable, and raises the question, "how can I be worthy of that?" That is your ego questioning the concept. Disregard it.

Life is a big deal. Enjoy it. All the tools to do so have been provided to you in this book.

The Contrarian's Guide to Natural Law

Many of us take life too seriously, especially when we are consciously working on self-improvement. The study of Natural Law can also seem pretty heavy. So here are some *lighter* aspects of life and living for your enjoyment:

Law of Mechanical Repair: After your hands become coated with grease, your nose will itch, or you will have to pee.

Law of the Workshop: Any tool, when dropped, will roll to the least accessible corner.

Law of Probability: The probability of being watched is directly proportional to the stupidity of your act.

Law of the Telephone: If you dial a wrong number, you never get a busy signal.

Law of the Alibi: If you tell the boss you were late for work because you had a flat tire, the very next morning you will have a flat tire.

Law of Variation: If you change lines at the store (or traffic lanes), the one you were in will start to move faster than the one you are in now.

Law of the Bath: When the body is fully immersed in water, the telephone will ring.

Law of Close Encounters: The probability of meeting someone you know increases dramatically when you are with someone you don't want to be seen with.

Law of Result: When you try to prove to someone that a machine won't work, it will.

Law of the Theater: At any event, the people whose seats are furthest from the aisle arrive last.

Law of Coffee: As soon as you sit down to a cup of hot coffee, your boss will ask you to do something which will last until the coffee is cold.

Murphy's Law of Lockers: If there are only two people in a locker room, they will have adjacent lockers.

Law of Rugs and Carpets: The chances of an open-faced jelly sandwich landing face down on a floor covering are directly correlated to the newness and cost of that carpet or rug.

Law of Logical Argument: Anything is possible if you don't know what you are talking about.

Brown's Law: If the shoe fits, it's ugly.

Oliver's Law: A closed mouth gathers no feet.

Wilson's Law: When you find a product that you really like, they will stop making it.

Doctor's Law: If you don't feel well, make an appointment to go to the doctor; by the time you get there, you'll feel better. Don't make an appointment and you will stay sick.

Law of Biomechanics: The severity of the itch is proportionally larger depending on where it is located and whether you can reach it or not.

Law of Illusion: About the time you think you see a light at the end of the tunnel, you discover it is only a train coming the other way.

Agnes Allen's Law: Almost anything is easier to get into than out of.

Army Axiom: Any order that can be misunderstood will be misunderstood.

Murphy's Law of Fools: It is impossible to make anything foolproof because fools are so ingenious.

First Law of Wing Walking: Never leave hold of something until you've got hold of something else.

Hull's Warning: Never insult an alligator until you have crossed the river.

Colson's Law: If you've got them by the balls, their hearts and minds will follow.

Canada Bill Jones' Law: A Smith & Wesson beats four aces.

Allen's Distinction: The lion and the calf shall lie down together, but the calf won't get much sleep.

Anthony's Law of Force: Don't force it; get a larger hammer.

Jacquin's Postulate: No man's life, liberty, or property are safe when the legislature is in session.

Bibliography & Additional Reading

Each of the books below has some references to Natural Law. Part of their value is that the information is expressed from different points of view, which I always think is a healthy thing for the serious student. Enjoy!

Holliwell, Raymond. *Working With the Law*. Camarillo: DeVorss & Company, 2005 Revised edition.

Michael, Emory. *The Alchemy of Sacred Living: Creating a Culture of Light*. Mountain Rose Publishing, 1998.

Milanovich, Norma and McCune, Shirley. *The Light Shall Set You Free*. Kalispell: Athena Publishing, 1996 Reprint edition.

Millman, Dan. *The Laws of Spirit: Simple, Powerful Truths for Making Life Work*. Tiburon: H.J. Kramer, 1995.

Three Initiates. *The Kabalion: A Study of the Hermetic Philosophy of Ancient Egypt and Greece*. Chicago: Yogi Publication Society, 1908.

Virtue, Doreen. *Divine Magic: The Seven Sacred Secrets of Manifestation*. (An updated version of the Kabalion). Carlsbad: Hay House, 1994.

Walsch, Neale Donald. *Conversations with God: An Uncommon Dialogue* (Book 3). London: Hodder & Stoughton, 1999.

Reference Works

Bletzer, June. *The Encyclopedic Psychic Dictionary*. Lithia Springs: New Leaf Distributing, 1998.

Davis, Andrew Jackson. *The Principles of Nature: Her Divine Revelations and a Voice to Mankind.* New York: S.S. Lyon, 1847.

Sam Inc. *Natural Law Governs: A Study Book.*

For those of you who truly take to Natural Law, you will understand the importance of mind, thought, and emotions to effectively using the laws to your greatest potentiality. I highly recommend some other books which will further enlighten you. Two are Eckhart Tolle's, *The Power of Now* and *A New Earth*. The third is a book which has been in almost constant publication since the second century A.D.: *Meditations of Marcus Aurelius*. Aurelius was a Stoic philosopher, an interest acquired during his Greek studies as a youth. You don't have to study Stoicism, but instead get an easy to read copy of his *Meditations* book, which will give you enough of a background through the writings of Aurelius to see how it all fits together.

Aurelius, Marcus and Hays, Gregory. *Meditations: A New Interpretation by Gregory Hays.* New York: Modern Library Paperbacks (A division of Random House Publishing), 2003.

Tolle, Eckhardt. *A New Earth: Awakening to your Life's Purpose.* London: Plume Books (A division of Penguin Group), 2005.

Tolle, Eckhardt. *The Power of Now: A Guide to Spiritual Enlightenment.* Novato: New World Library, 1999.

About Rev. Ryan

Terry Ryan has had two parallel paths throughout much of his life: one working in the nonprofit world in the fight against the AIDS epidemic, and the other studies in the spiritual, occult, and metaphysical areas. Each path assisted his personal growth and spiritual unfoldment, while providing a positive cross-over effect on each other.

He was born and raised in Grand Rapids, Michigan. In the late 1970's he moved to the Detroit, Michigan area where he still lives. In September 1985, he began volunteering for the first HIV/AIDS nonprofit organization in Michigan, and in 1986 was hired as its office manager. During his 35 year career, he served in multiple roles, including Executive Director at the Michigan AIDS Coalition. Now retired, Terry devotes his time to his metaphysical and mediumistic studies, teaching, and writing.

Terry became acquainted with Camp Chesterfield in Indiana in 1983, and, with a group of friends, made an exploratory trip there. He began studies at Camp in 1983 and was Ordained in 2000 as a Spiritualist Minister. He has been a Resident Medium and Teacher at Camp since 1995. In addition to teaching at Camp Chesterfield, Terry has taught classes and workshops throughout numerous cities in the Midwest United States, and he continues to teach psychic development classes in metro Detroit. Terry is also a self-avowed Stoic, as that philosophy aligns well with Natural Law studies and pursuits, which are his great passion.

"There are three kinds of people in the world.

Those who make things happen.

Those who watch things happen.

Those who wonder what happened."

~ Anonymous

Ordering Information

For individual copies of this book:

www.Amazon.com

For resale case lot orders, contact your local book wholesaler through Ingram or Baker & Taylor.

For speaking and seminar opportunities, contact Rev. Ryan at:

www.RevTerryRyan.com

Ordering Information

For individual copies of this book:

www.Amazon.com

For resale case lot orders, contact your local book wholesaler through Ingram or Baker & Taylor.

For speaking and seminar opportunities, contact Rev. Ryan at:

www.RevTerryRyan.com

Made in the USA
Monee, IL
15 March 2021

62871983R00073